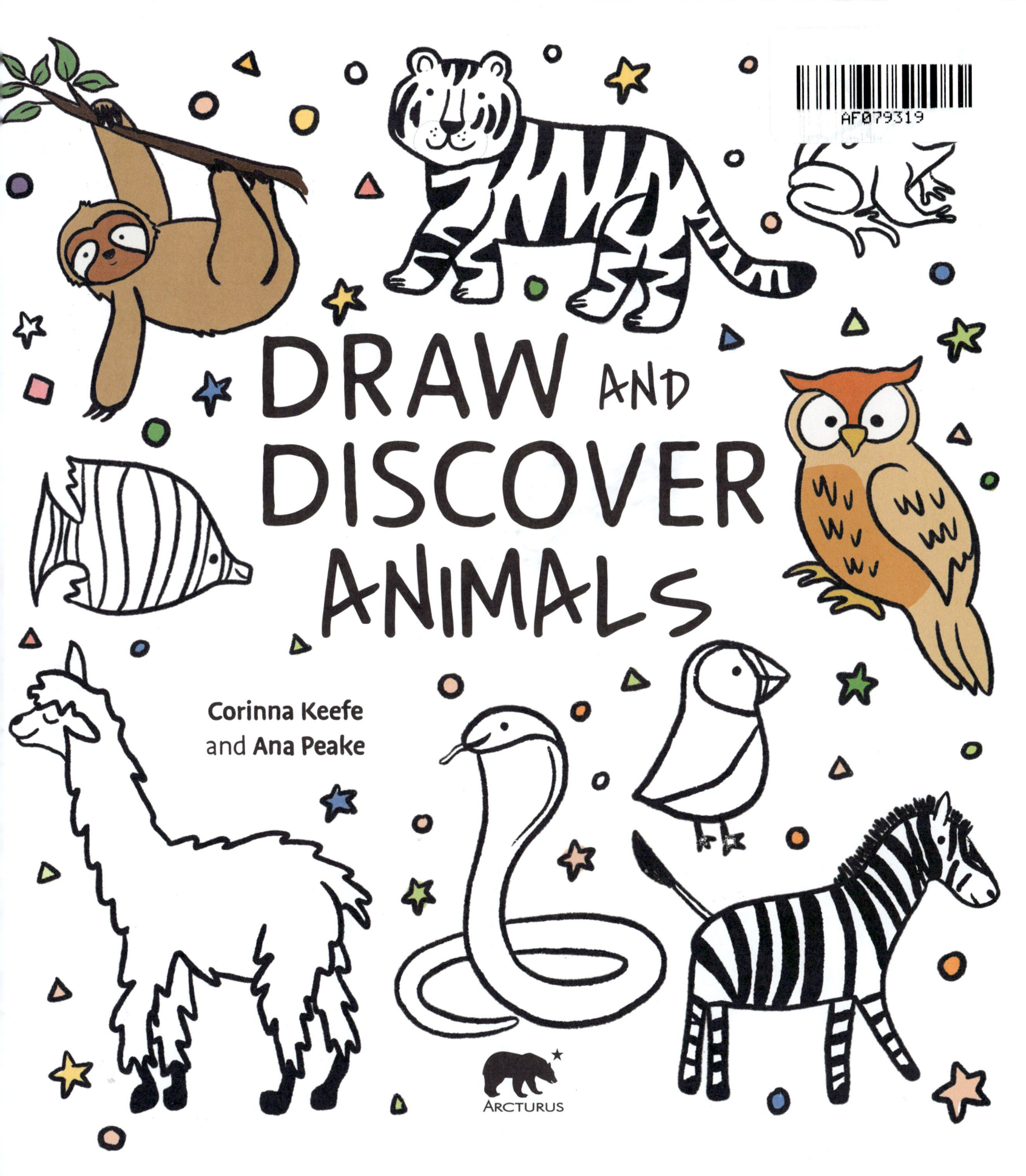

This edition published in 2024 by Arcturus Publishing Limited,
26/27 Bickels Yard, 151–153 Bermondsey Street, London SE1 3HA

Copyright © Arcturus Holdings Limited

All rights reserved. No part of this publication may be reproduced, stored in a retrieval system, or transmitted, in any form or by any means, electronic, mechanical, photocopying, recording, or otherwise, without prior written permission in accordance with the provisions of the Copyright Act 1956 (as amended). Any person or persons who do any unauthorized act in relation to this publication may be liable to criminal prosecution and civil claims for damages.

Author: Corinna Keefe
Illustrator: Ana Peake
Editor: Violet Peto
Designer: Stefan Holliland
Managing Editor: Joe Harris

ISBN: 978-1-3988-2866-7
CH011059NT
Supplier 29, Date 1123, PI 00004295

Printed in China

Eye spy
Owls have different eyelids for blinking, sleeping, and cleaning their eyes.

What a hoot
They don't just hoot—some can screech, whistle, rattle, hiss, or even bark!

Fancy feet
An owl's feet have toes facing forward and backward!

Sneaking around
Owls have special feathers that allow them to hunt prey quietly.

All About Owls

★ Owls are meat-eaters, meaning that they eat other animals. To find their food, owls rely on their very good eyesight.

★ Unlike humans, owls have tube-shaped eyes! These help them see really far.

How to Draw an Angelfish

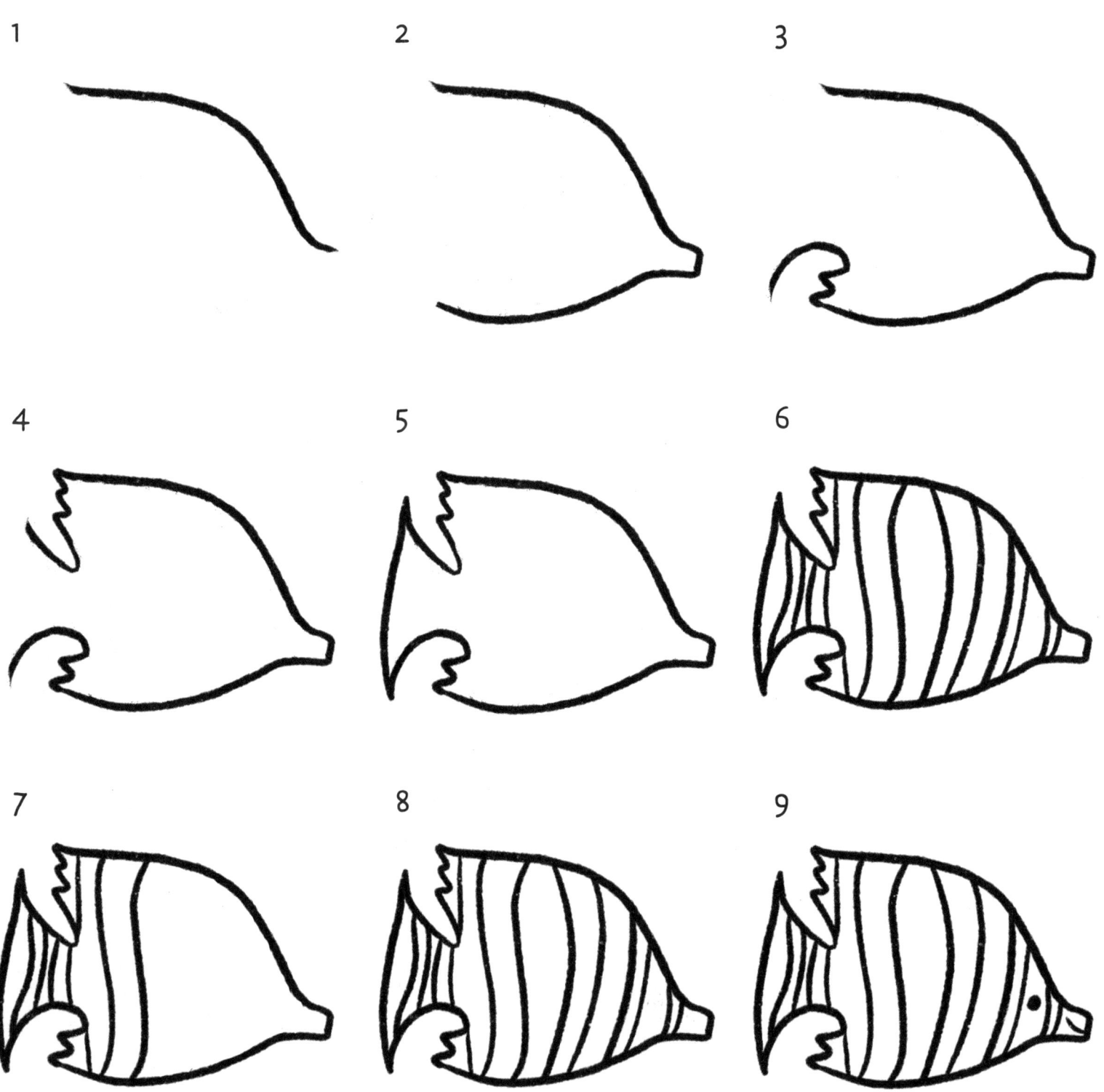

How to Draw ...

A Chameleon ... 4–5	A Turkey ... 36–37	A Clownfish ... 68–69
An Owl ... 6–7	A Gecko ... 38–39	A Raccoon ... 70–71
An Angelfish ... 8–9	A Wolf ... 40–41	A Flamingo ... 72–73
A Sloth ... 10–11	A Gorilla ... 42–43	A Crab ... 74–75
A Puffin ... 12–13	A Seahorse ... 44–45	A Horse ... 76–77
A Cat ... 14–15	A Polar Bear ... 46–47	An Ostrich ... 78–79
A Brown Bear ... 16–17	A Bat ... 48–49	A Platypus ... 80–81
A Pelican ... 18–19	A Rhino ... 50–51	An Alpaca ... 82–83
A Shark ... 20–21	A Hedgehog ... 52–53	A Monkey ... 84–85
A Deer ... 22–23	A Tiger ... 54–55	A Turtle ... 86–87
A Kiwi ... 24–25	A Dolphin ... 56–57	A Fox ... 88–89
A Frog ... 26–27	A Koala ... 58–59	An Elephant ... 90–91
A Zebra ... 28–29	An Eagle ... 60–61	A Beaver ... 92–93
A Squirrel ... 30–31	A Snake ... 62–63	A Panda ... 94–95
An Octopus ... 32–33	A Giraffe ... 64–65	
A Crocodile ... 34–35	A Rabbit ... 66–67	

How to Draw a Chameleon

Zap!
Chameleons catch food with their long, fast-moving tongues.

Double vision
A chameleon can move its big eyes separately and look in two directions at once.

Up high
Many chameleons like this one live in trees.

Steady ...
Its long, curling tail helps the chameleon balance and hold on in the trees.

All About Chameleons
★ Chameleons change the shade of their skin for communication, camouflage (hiding by looking like the things around you), and to show their emotions.

How to Draw an Owl

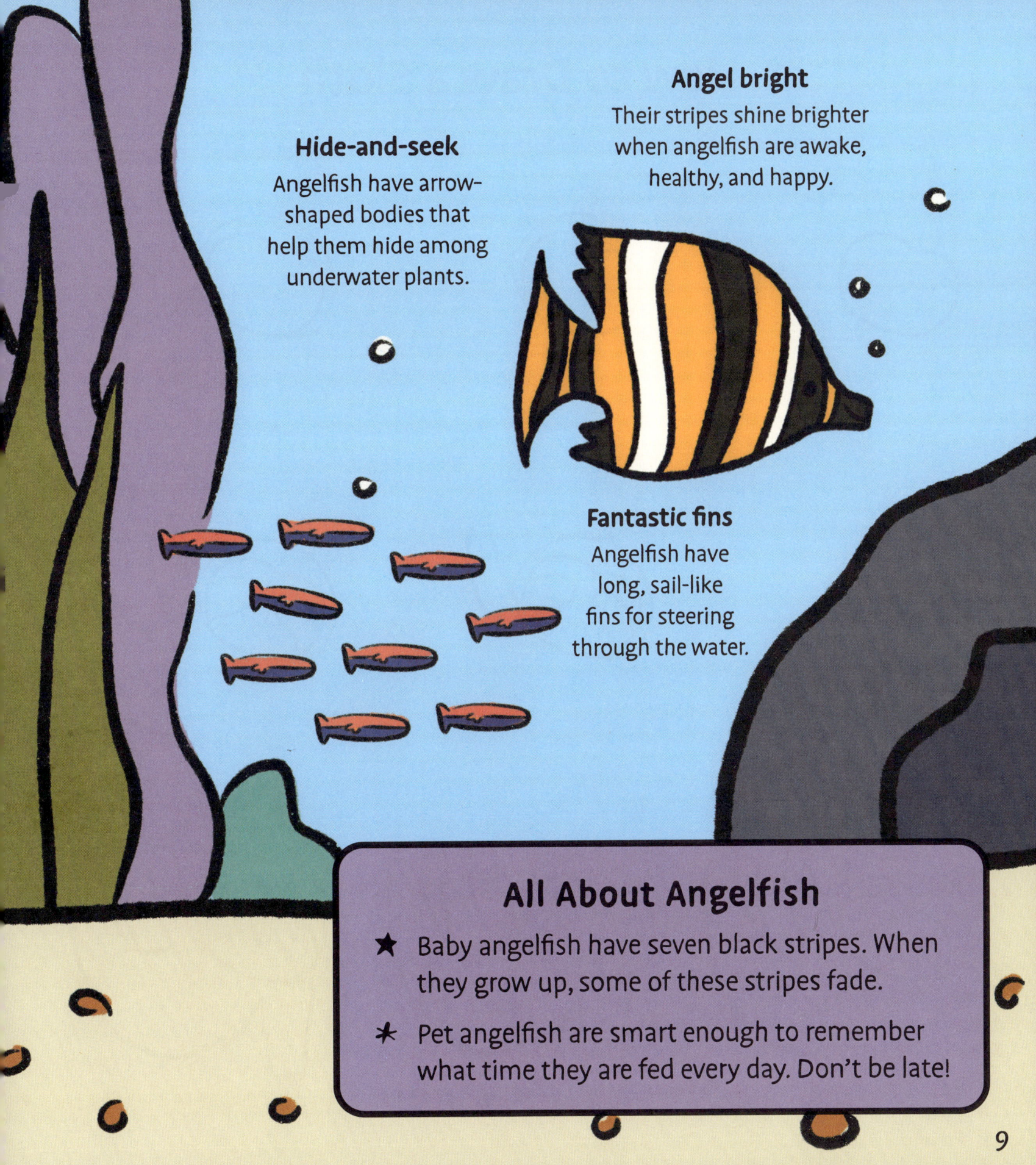

Hide-and-seek
Angelfish have arrow-shaped bodies that help them hide among underwater plants.

Angel bright
Their stripes shine brighter when angelfish are awake, healthy, and happy.

Fantastic fins
Angelfish have long, sail-like fins for steering through the water.

All About Angelfish

★ Baby angelfish have seven black stripes. When they grow up, some of these stripes fade.

✱ Pet angelfish are smart enough to remember what time they are fed every day. Don't be late!

How to Draw a Sloth

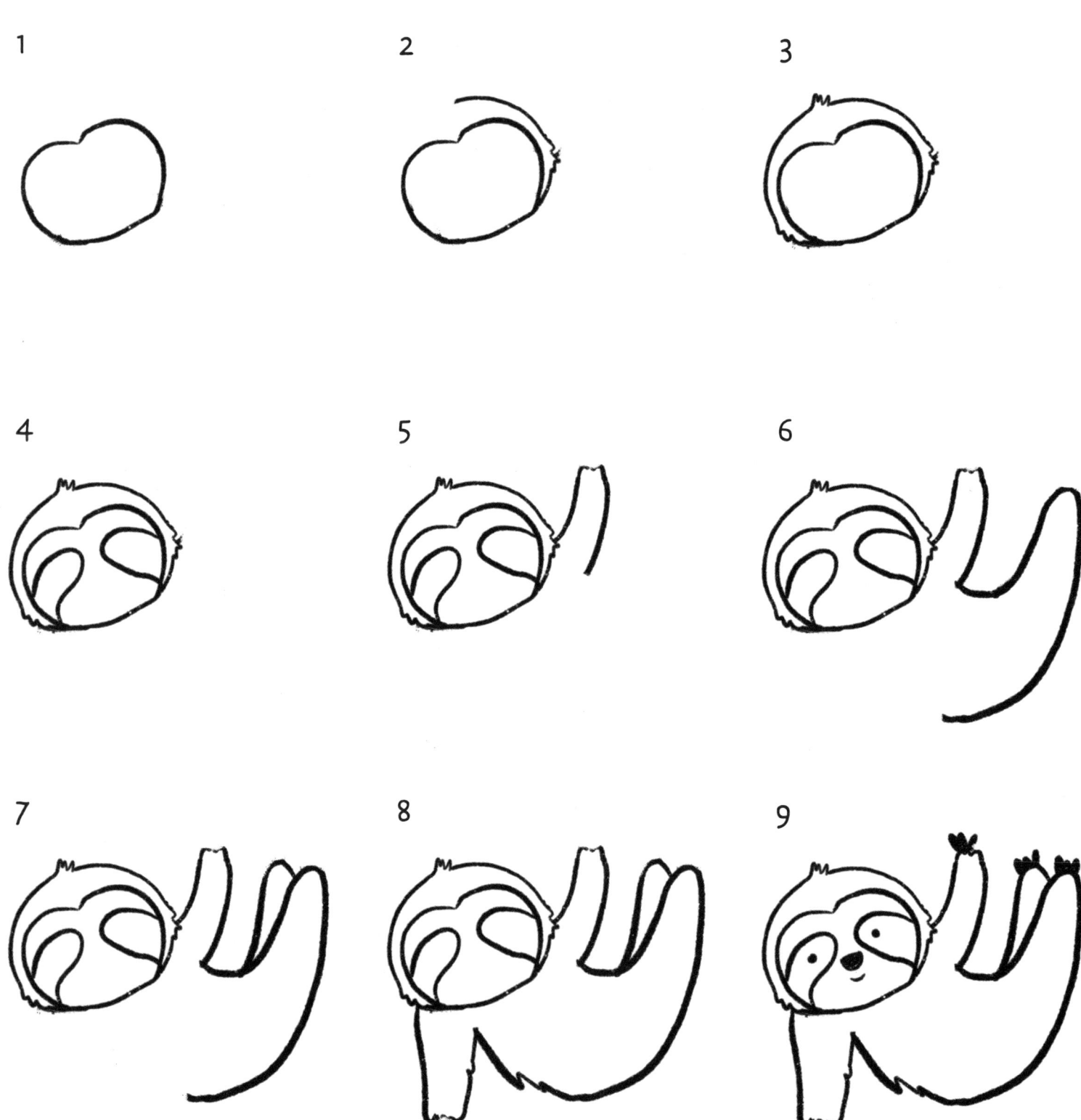

Fur friends
Sloths have green stuff called algae on their fur. This helps them hide. They can also snack on it!

Counting toes
This is a three-toed sloth. It has three long claws on its front and back legs.

Hold on!
Sloths can lock their hands and feet in place to hang upside down for hours!

All About Sloths
* Sloths can sleep for up to 20 hours a day. No wonder the word *sloth* means "laziness!"

How to Draw a Puffin

1
2
3
4
5
6
7
8
9

Beautiful beaks
Puffins are famous for their brightly striped beaks.

Water wings
Puffins' short, strong wings are perfect for "flying" underwater.

Somewhere safe
Puffins lay their eggs in earth burrows or cracks in the rock.

All About Puffins

★ Because of their bright beaks, puffins are also called sea parrots or sea clowns!

★ Puffins live at sea in the colder months. They only land in the spring and summer.

How to Draw a Cat

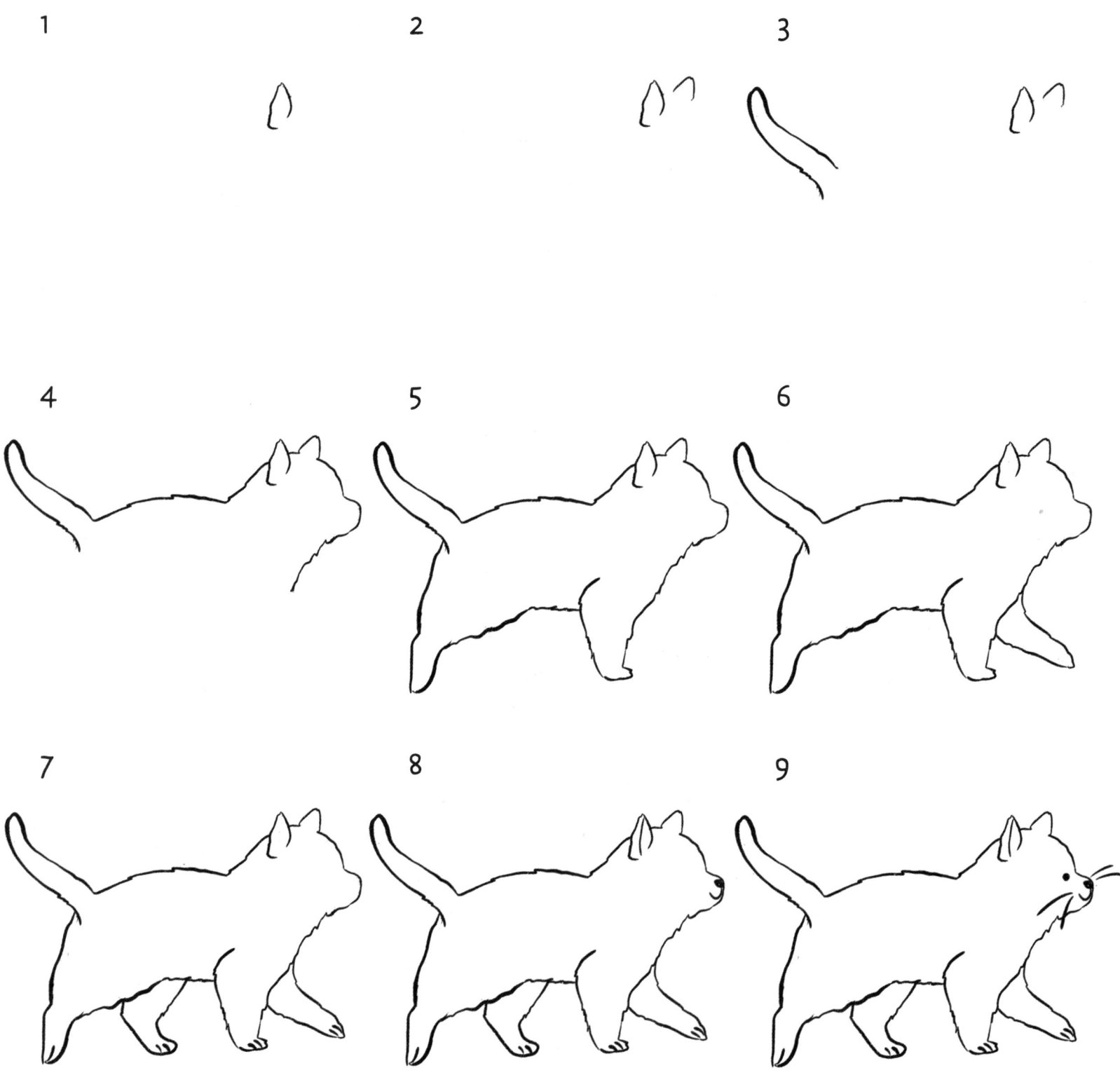

How to Draw a Brown Bear

All About Bears

★ Brown bears sleep through the winter. They eat a lot of food before then, so that they won't get hungry until spring.

✳ Brown bears are good at fishing. They catch fish with their paws or dive into the water and chase them!

Sharp ears
This bear can hear twice as well as a human. It can hear better than it can see.

Watch out!
A brown bear has long, sharp claws.

What's for dinner?
Brown bears can eat up to 40 kg (90 lb) of food a day. That's about the weight of eight watermelons!

How to Draw a Pelican

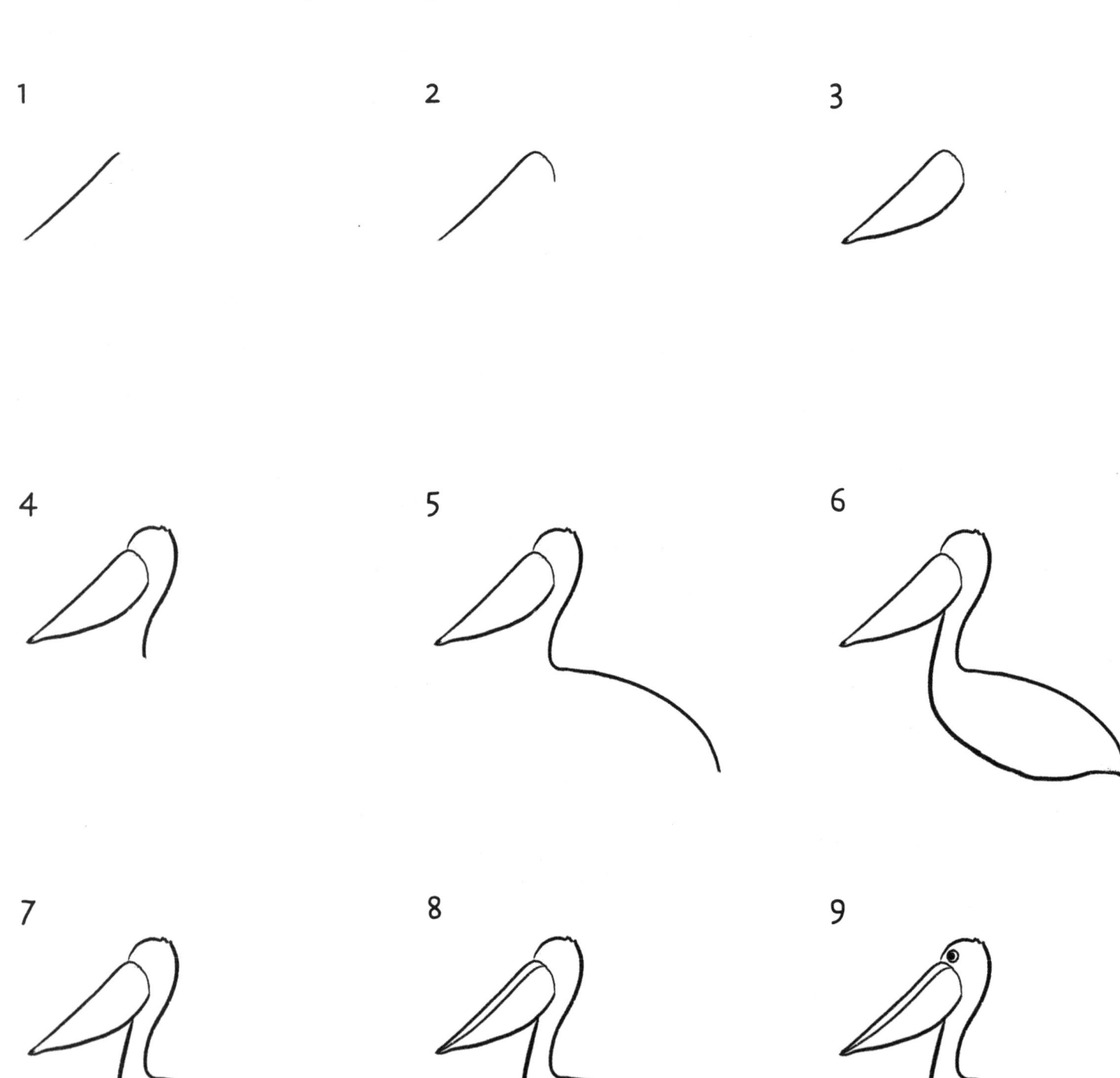

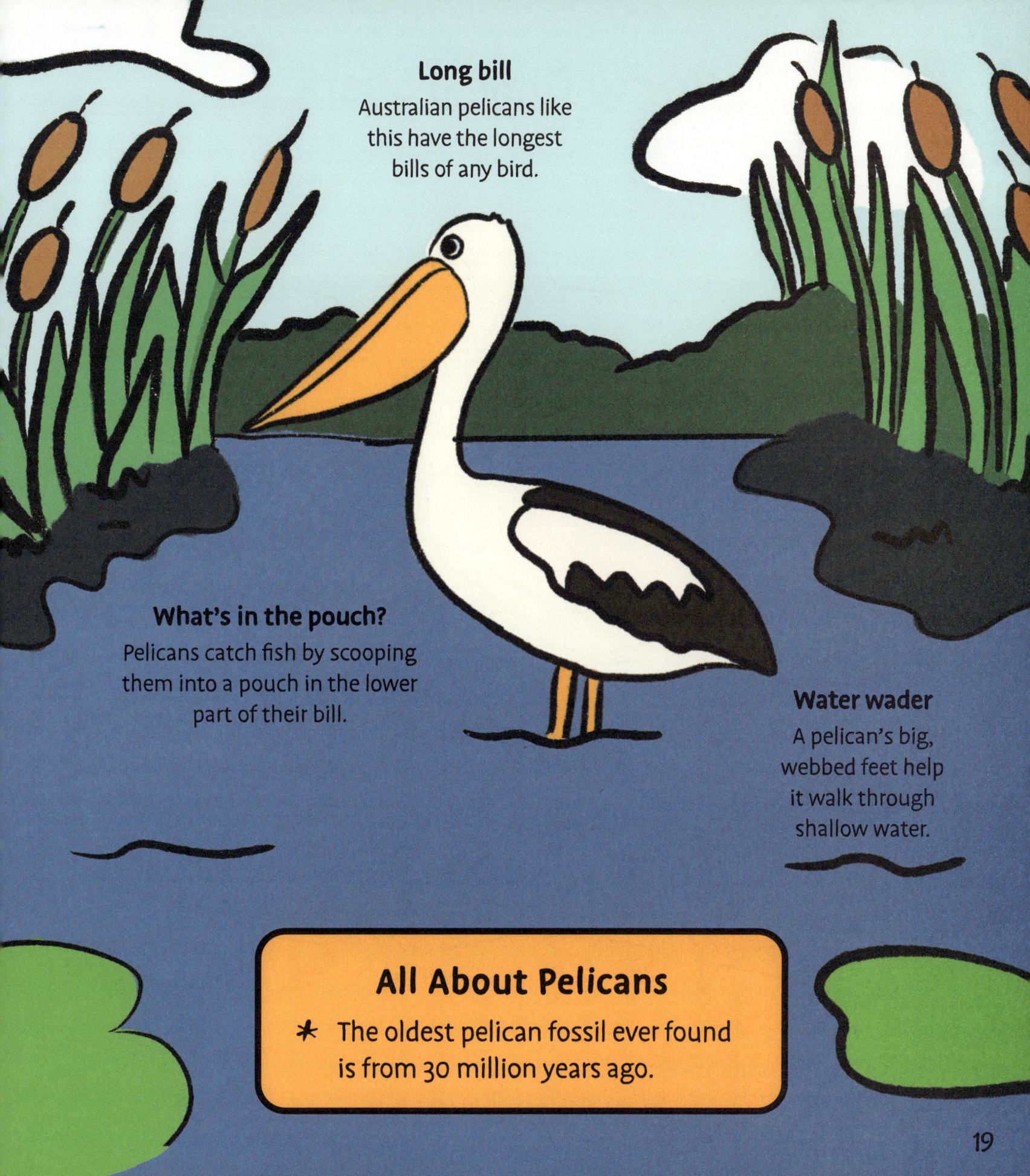

How to Draw a Shark

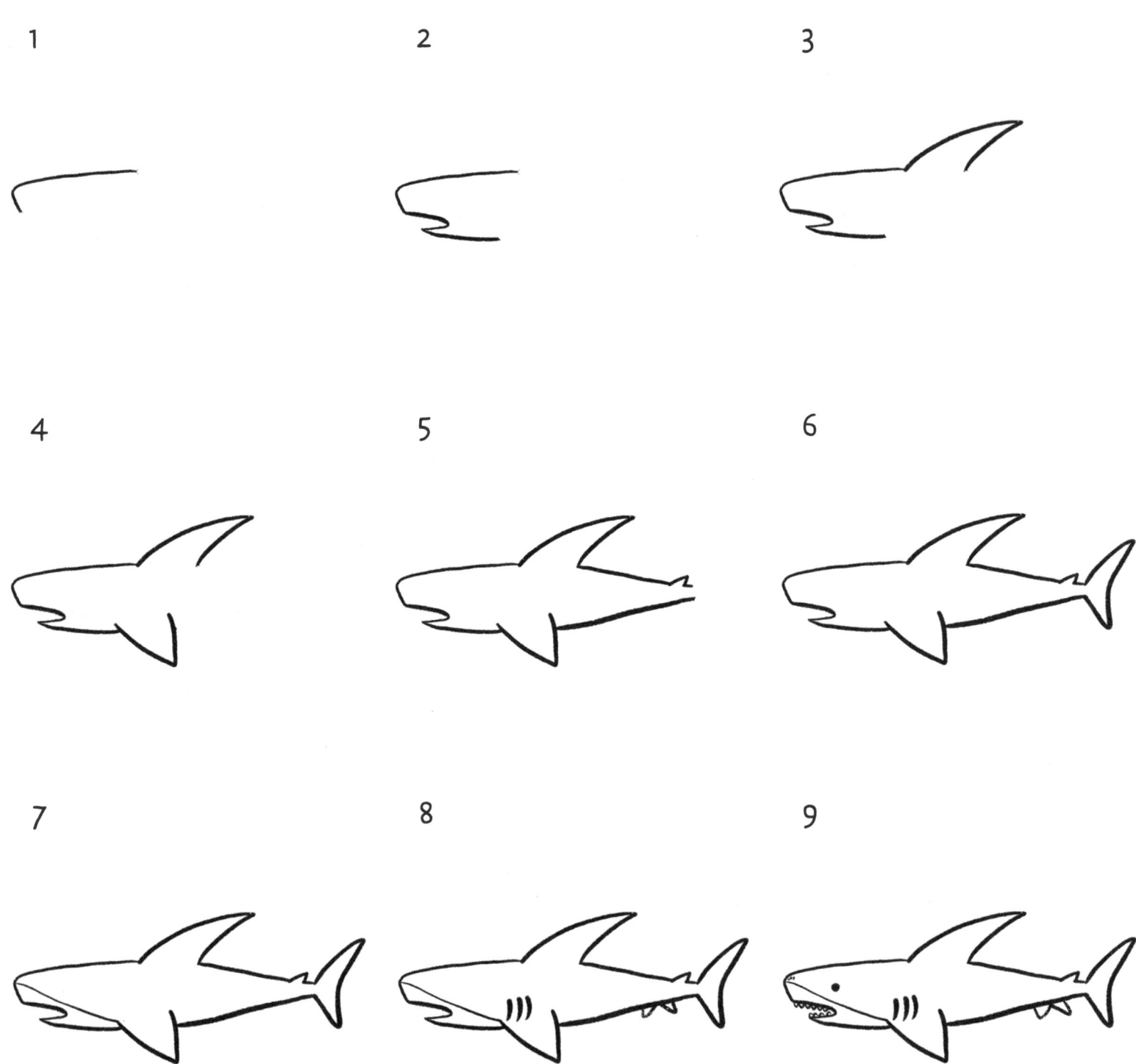

Super senses
A shark has sensors on its head. It uses them to find its way and its food.

What kind of shark?
Blue sharks like this one have a slim body and extra-long front fins.

Night sight
Sharks have a special layer in their eyes that helps them see in the dark.

All About Sharks

★ 97 percent of shark species don't hurt humans ... even if they look a little bit scary!

★ You can put a shark in a trance by flipping it on its back. Scientists use this trick when they want to look at a shark more closely.

How to Draw a Deer

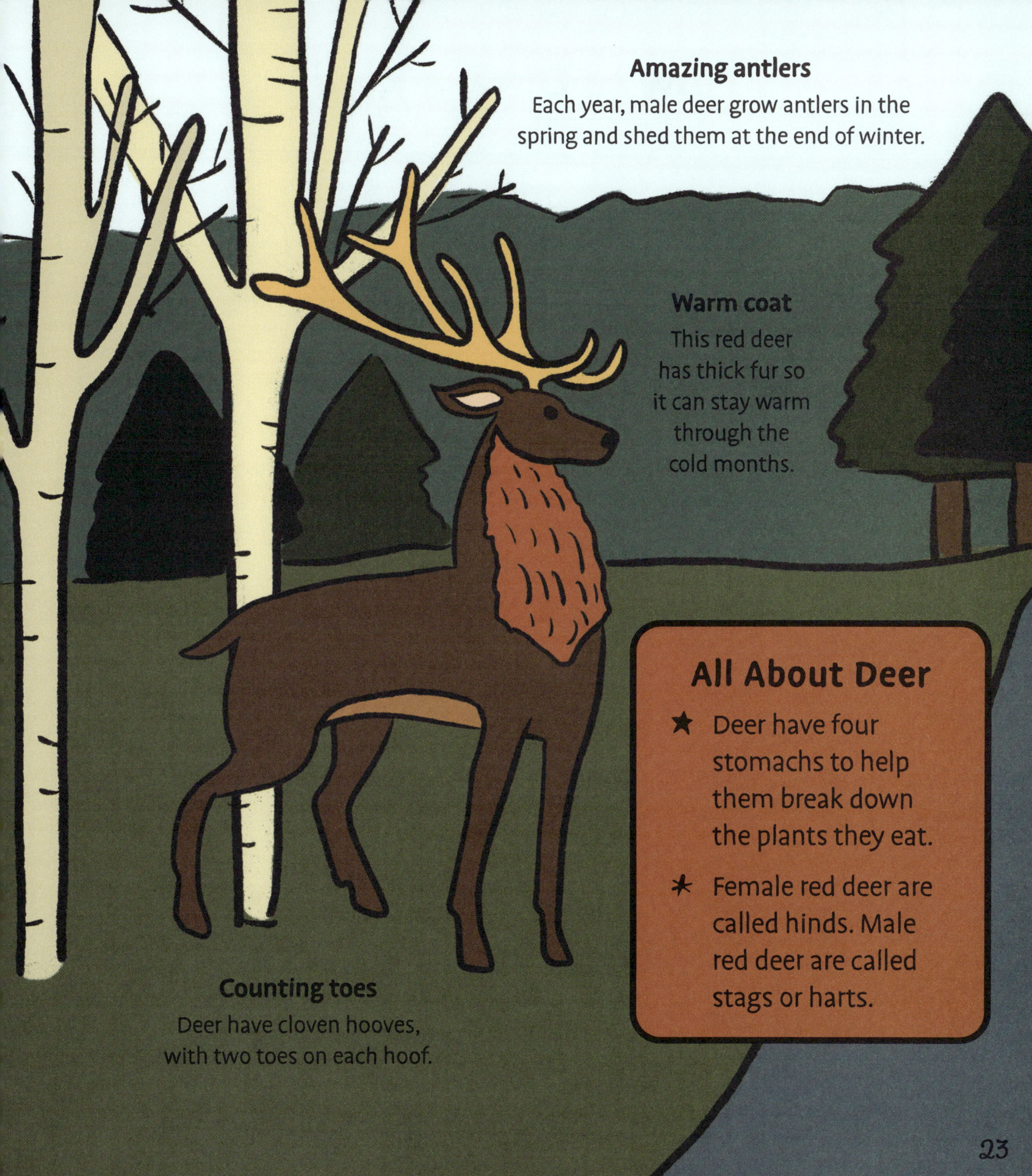

Amazing antlers
Each year, male deer grow antlers in the spring and shed them at the end of winter.

Warm coat
This red deer has thick fur so it can stay warm through the cold months.

Counting toes
Deer have cloven hooves, with two toes on each hoof.

All About Deer

★ Deer have four stomachs to help them break down the plants they eat.

✱ Female red deer are called hinds. Male red deer are called stags or harts.

How to Draw a Kiwi

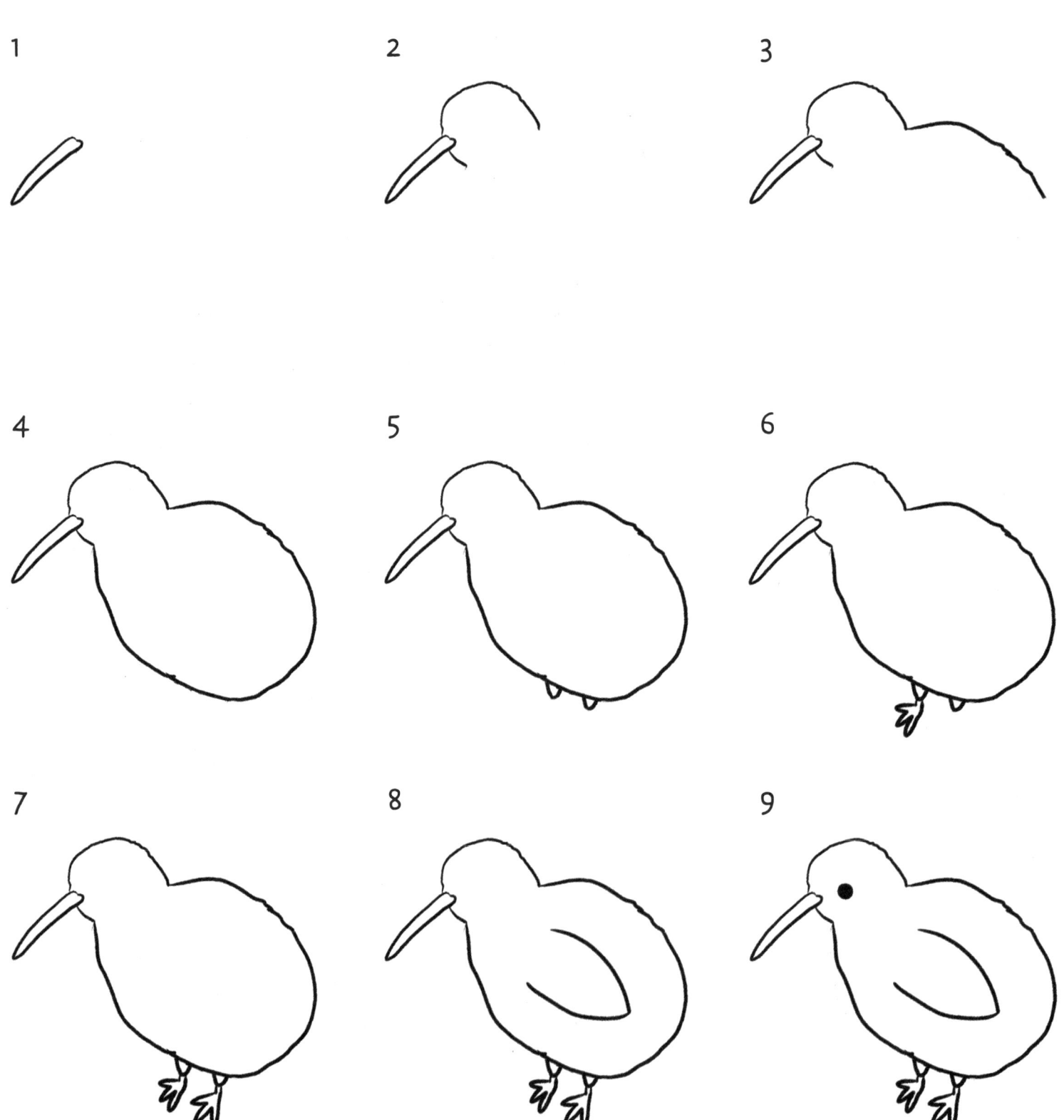

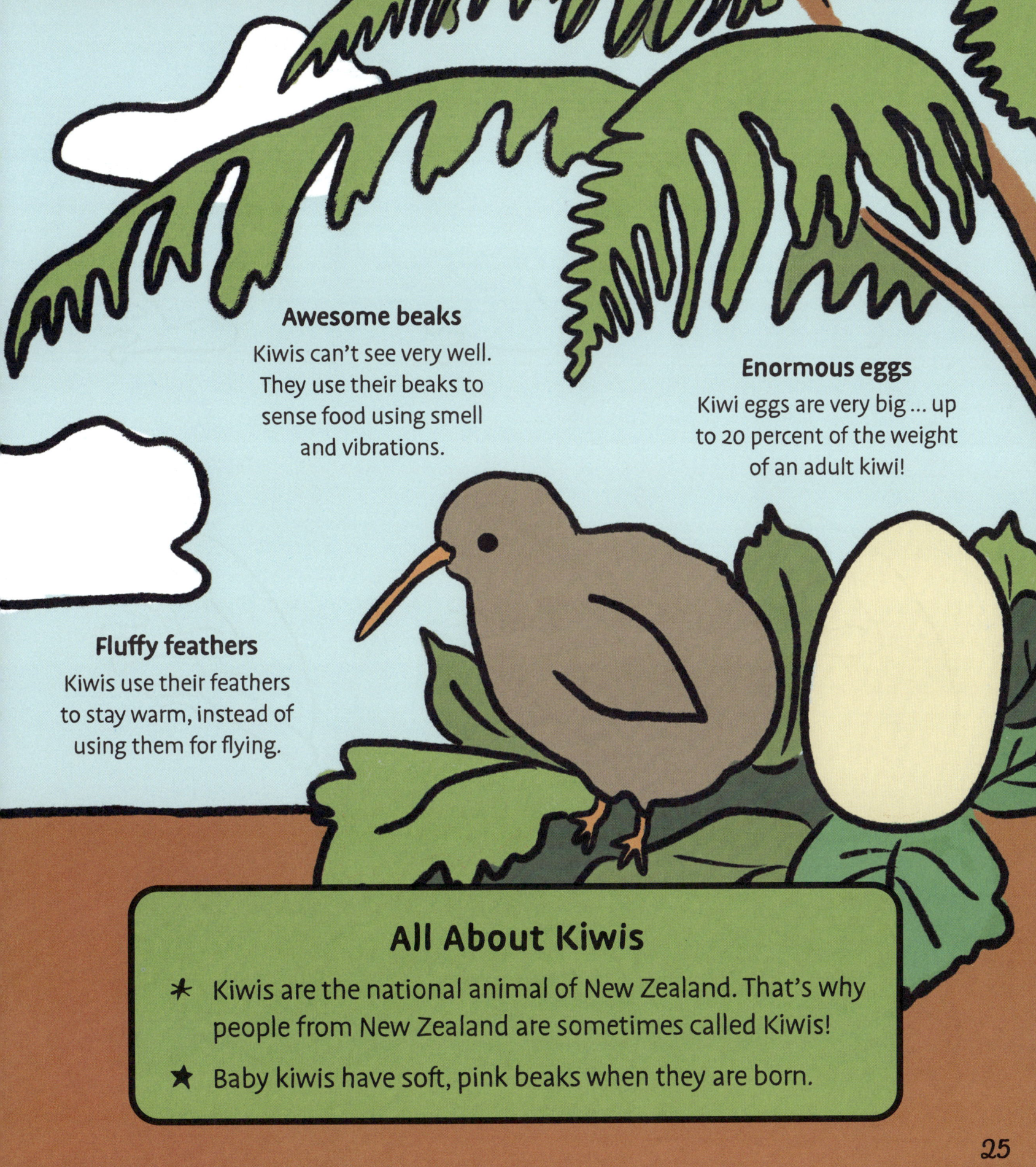

Awesome beaks
Kiwis can't see very well. They use their beaks to sense food using smell and vibrations.

Enormous eggs
Kiwi eggs are very big ... up to 20 percent of the weight of an adult kiwi!

Fluffy feathers
Kiwis use their feathers to stay warm, instead of using them for flying.

All About Kiwis

★ Kiwis are the national animal of New Zealand. That's why people from New Zealand are sometimes called Kiwis!

★ Baby kiwis have soft, pink beaks when they are born.

How to Draw a Frog

1
2
3
4
5
6
7
8
9

26

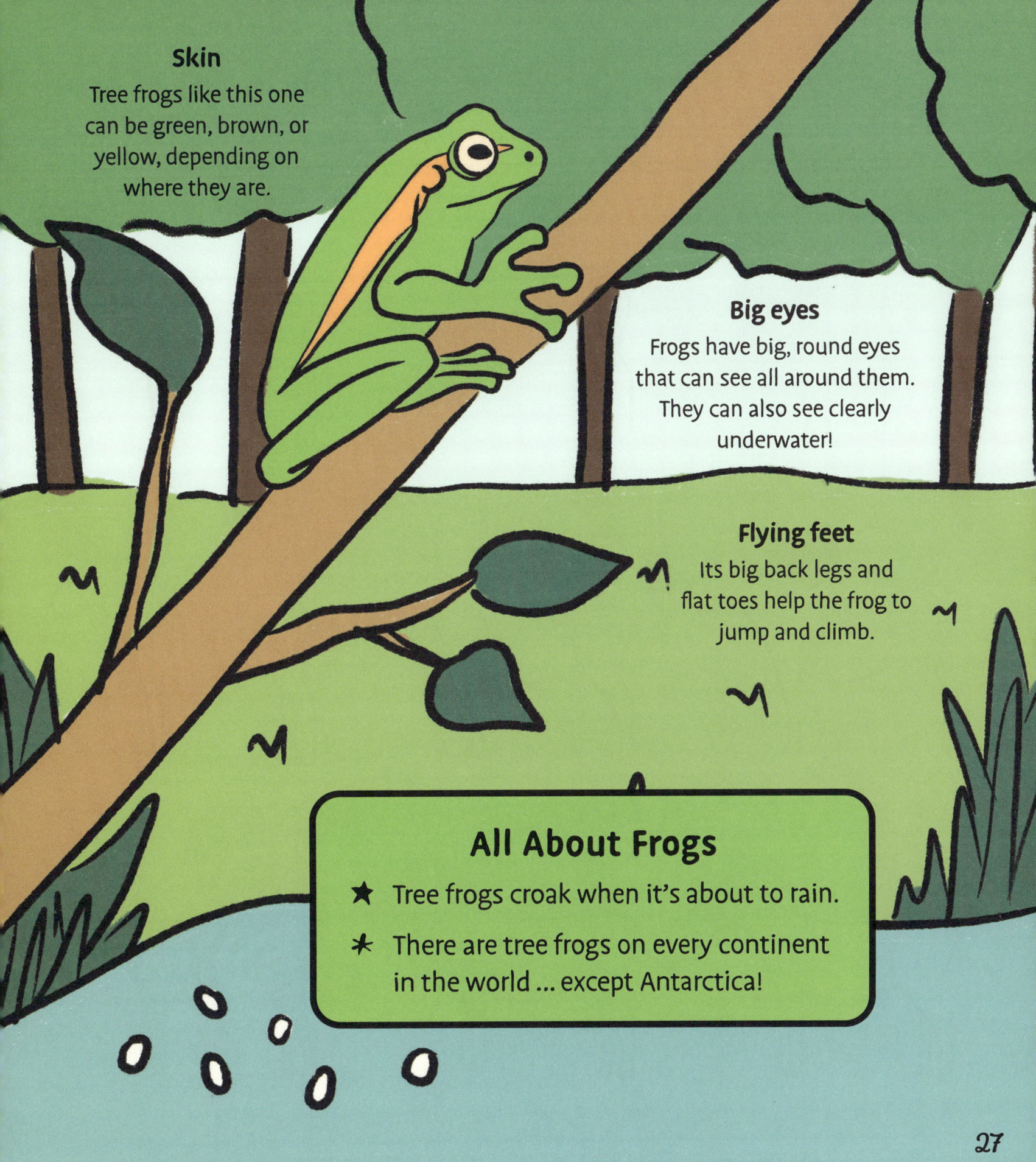

How to Draw a Zebra

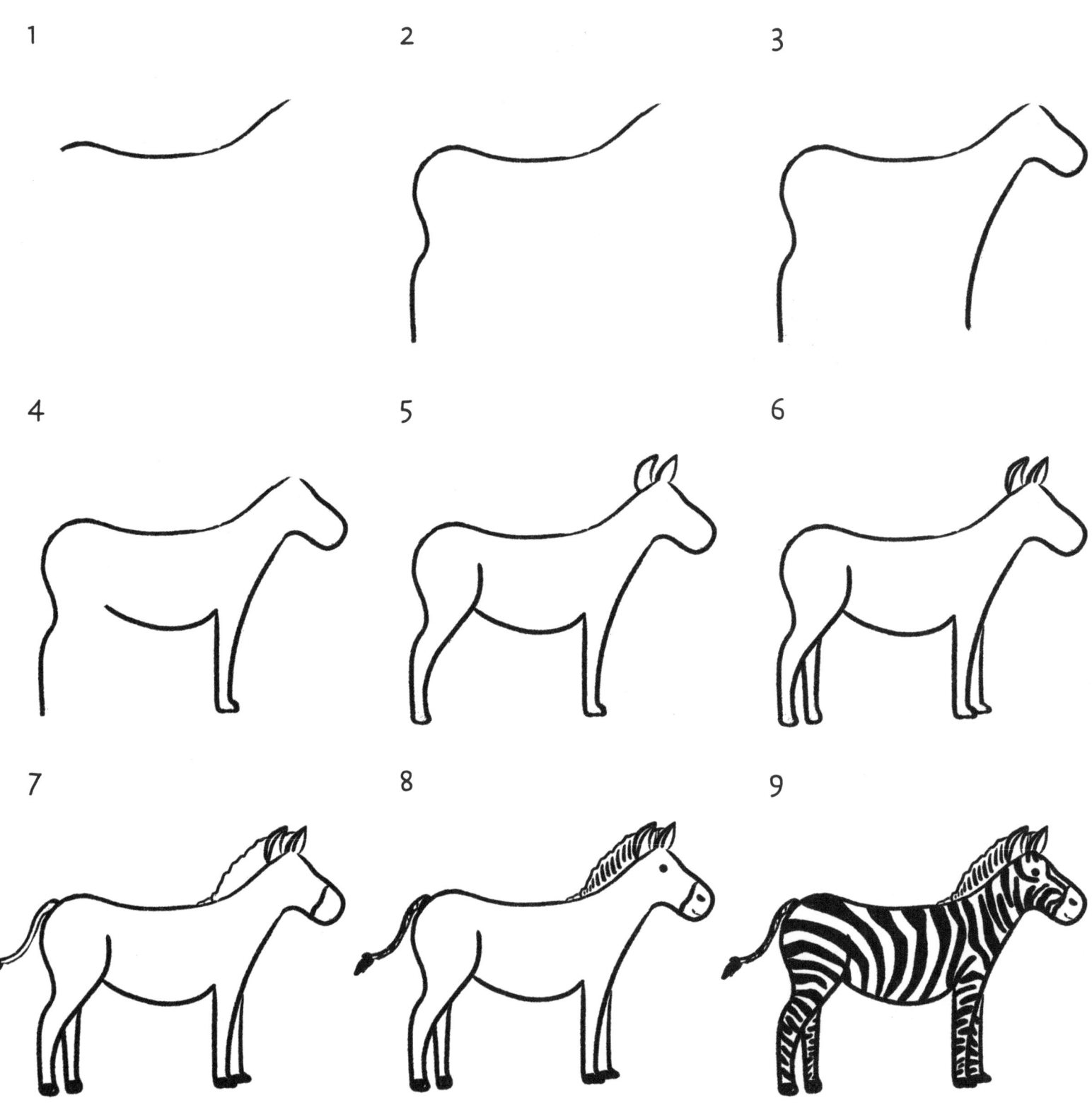

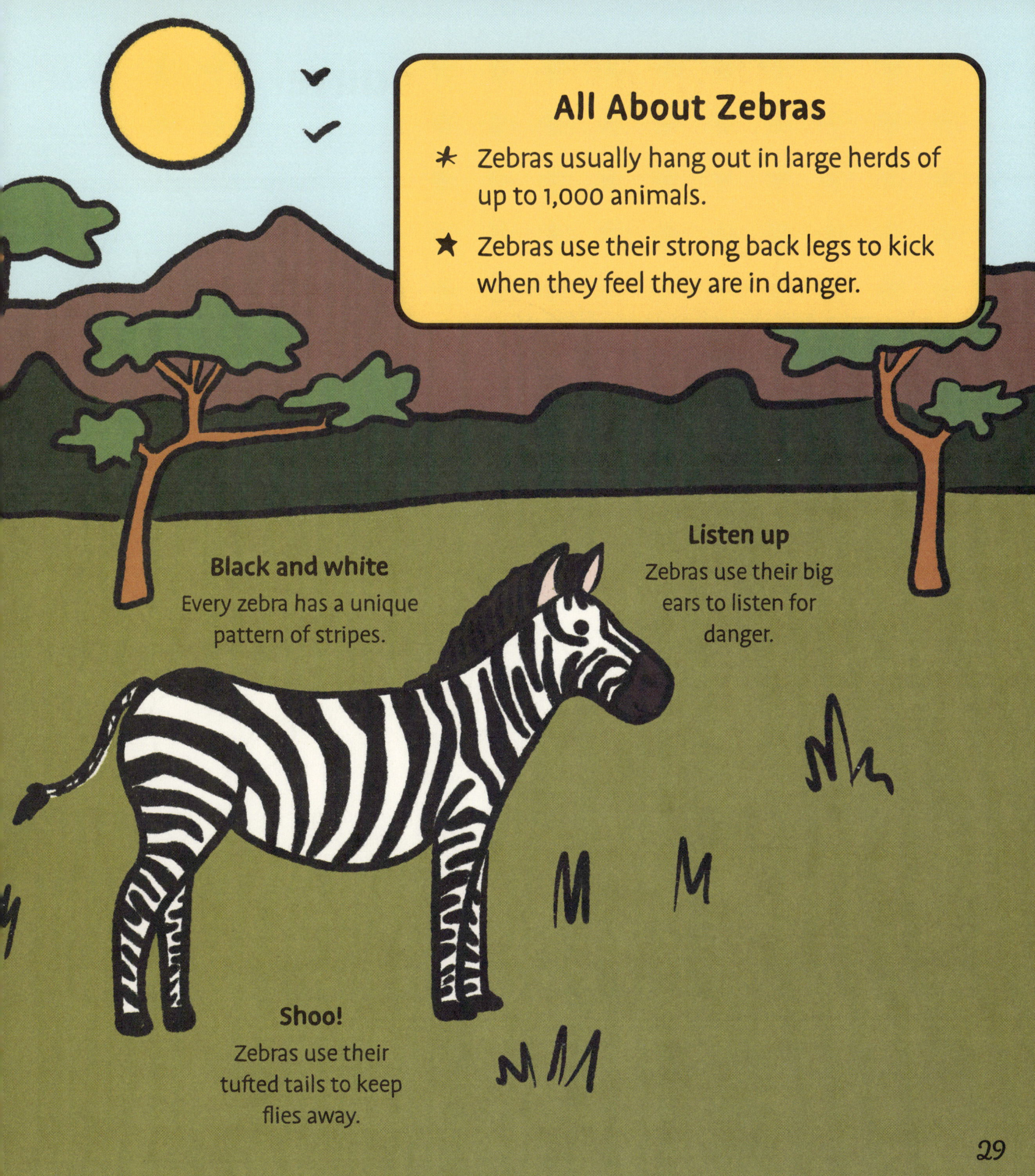

How to Draw a Squirrel

All About Squirrels

★ Squirrels are really good at collecting and storing food.

✶ They have special pouches in their cheeks for holding nuts, seeds, and berries.

Tall tails
Squirrels use their bushy tails to balance, for shelter, and to signal to other squirrels.

Nutty nibblers
They have strong front teeth so that they can bite tough nuts and seeds.

Wow!
Squirrels can point their feet backward to run down trees head first!

How to Draw an Octopus

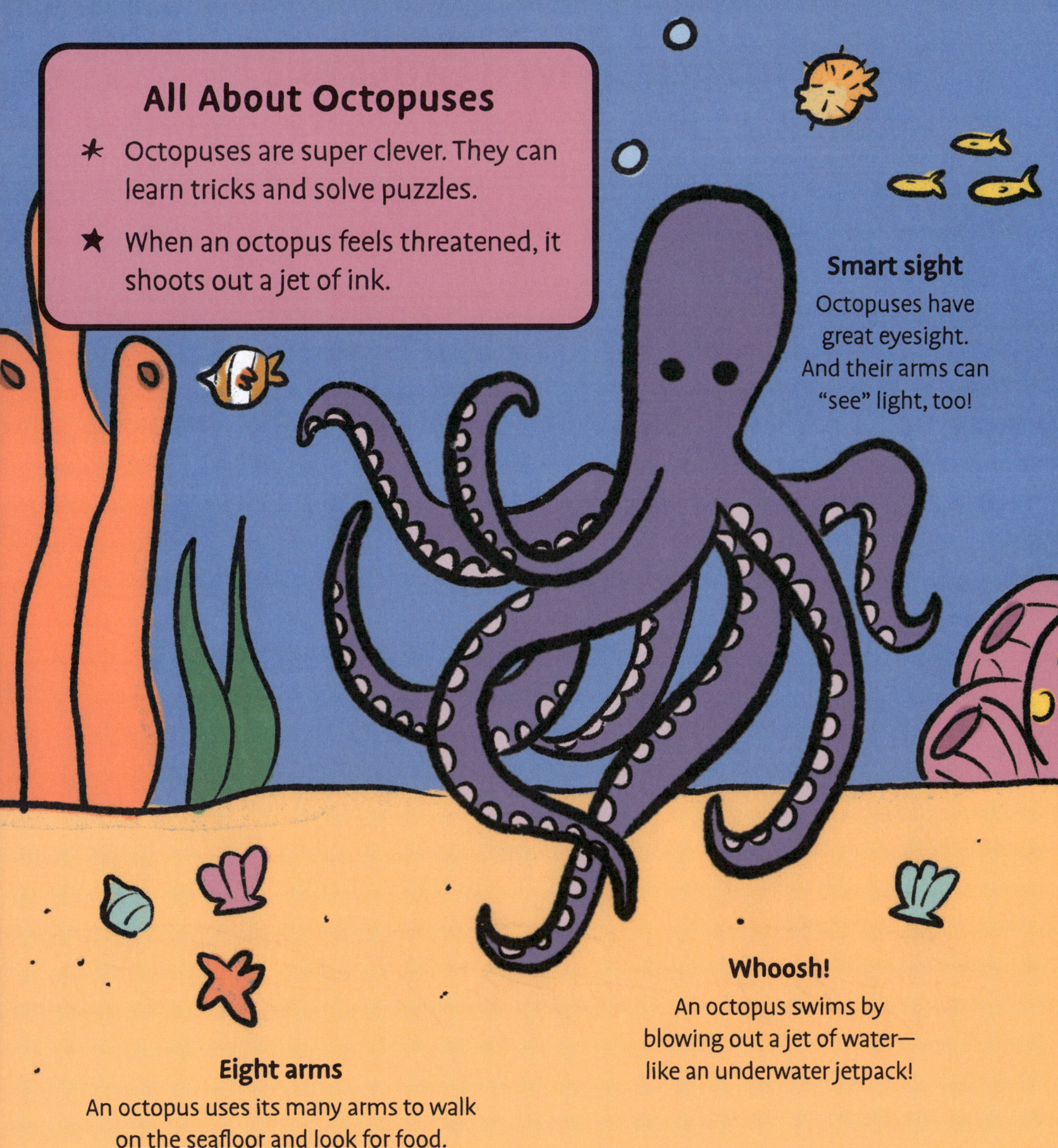

All About Octopuses

★ Octopuses are super clever. They can learn tricks and solve puzzles.

★ When an octopus feels threatened, it shoots out a jet of ink.

Smart sight
Octopuses have great eyesight. And their arms can "see" light, too!

Eight arms
An octopus uses its many arms to walk on the seafloor and look for food.

Whoosh!
An octopus swims by blowing out a jet of water—like an underwater jetpack!

How to Draw a Crocodile

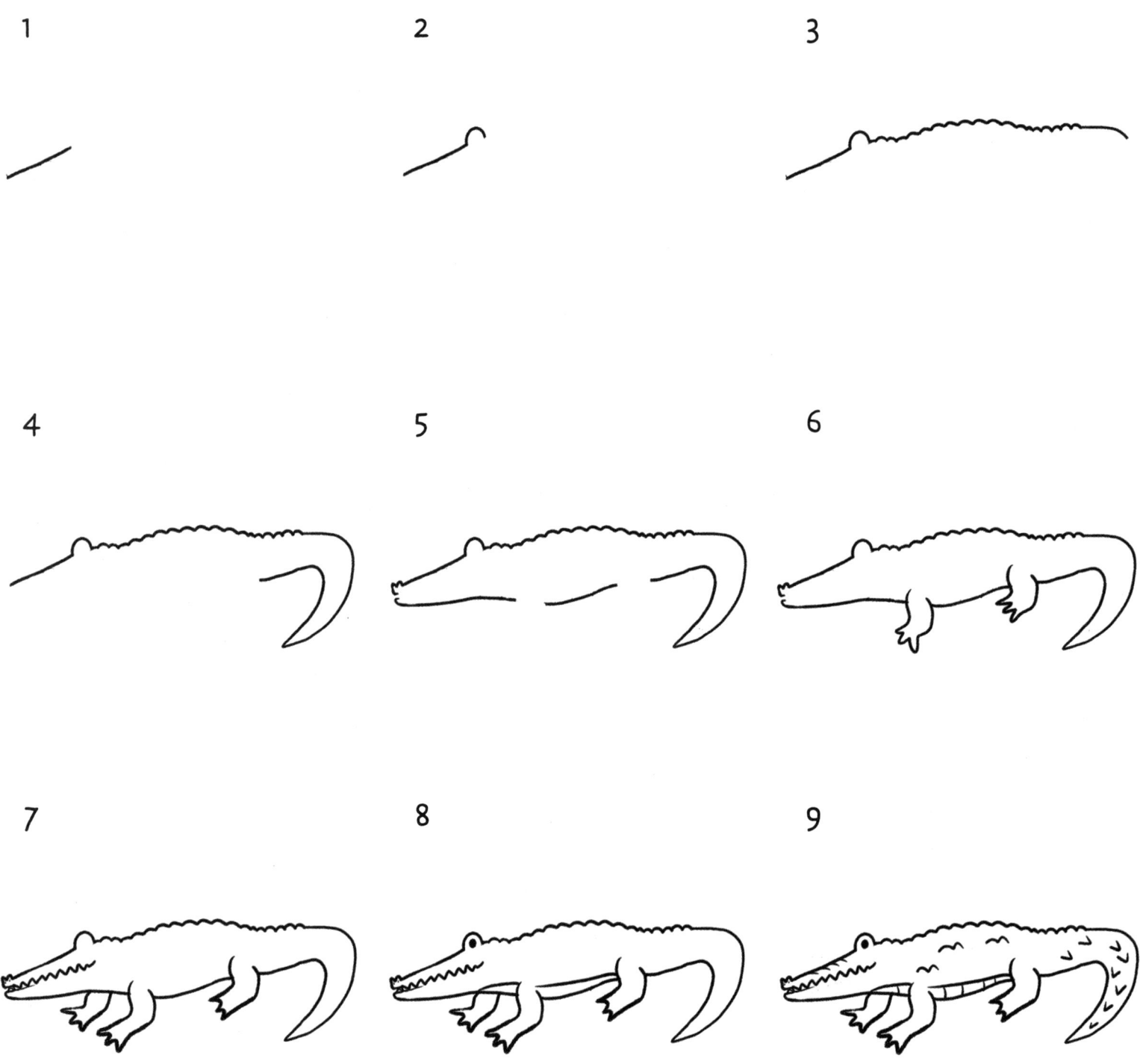

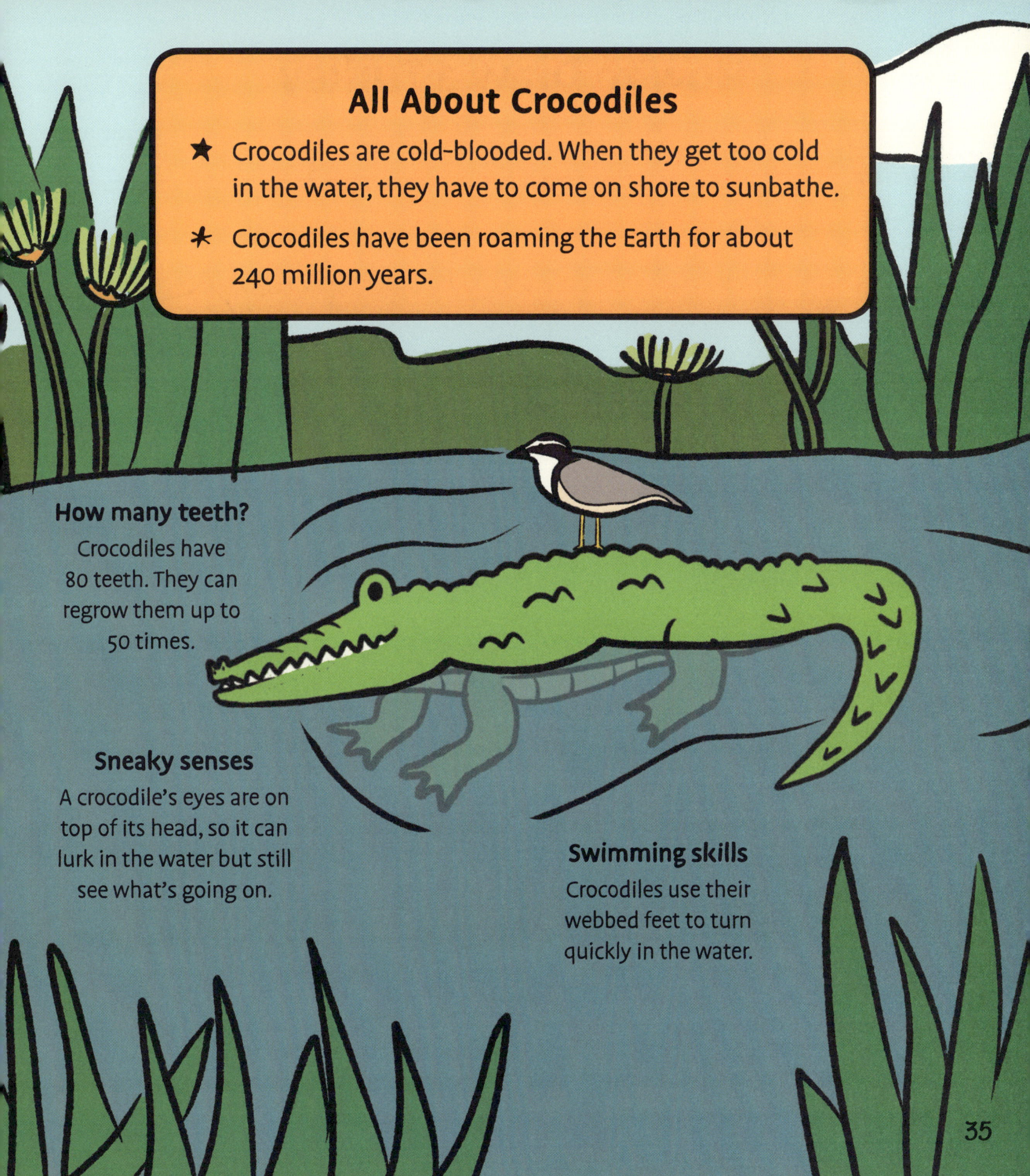

All About Crocodiles

★ Crocodiles are cold-blooded. When they get too cold in the water, they have to come on shore to sunbathe.

★ Crocodiles have been roaming the Earth for about 240 million years.

How many teeth?
Crocodiles have 80 teeth. They can regrow them up to 50 times.

Sneaky senses
A crocodile's eyes are on top of its head, so it can lurk in the water but still see what's going on.

Swimming skills
Crocodiles use their webbed feet to turn quickly in the water.

How to Draw a Turkey

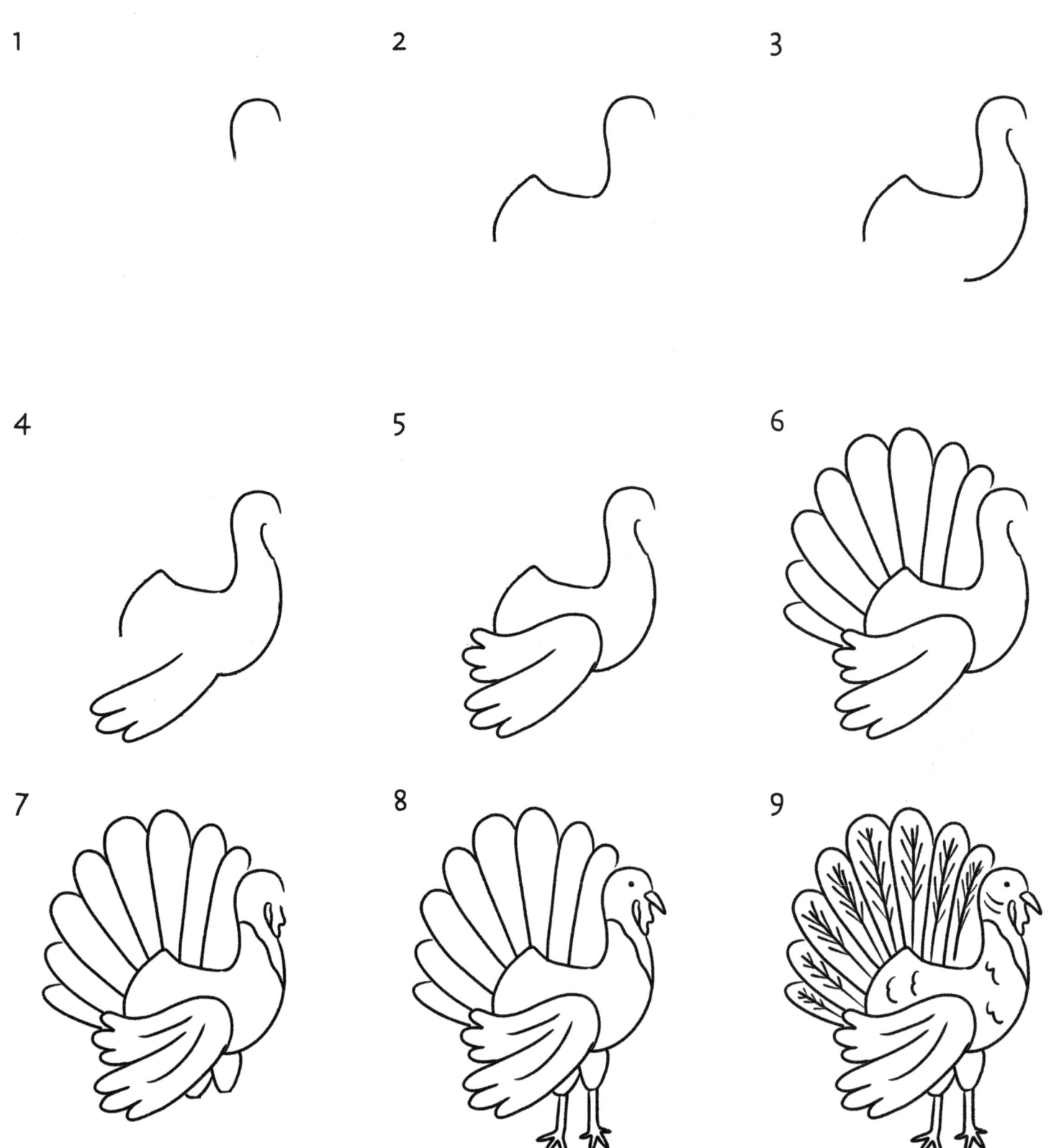

How to Draw a Gecko

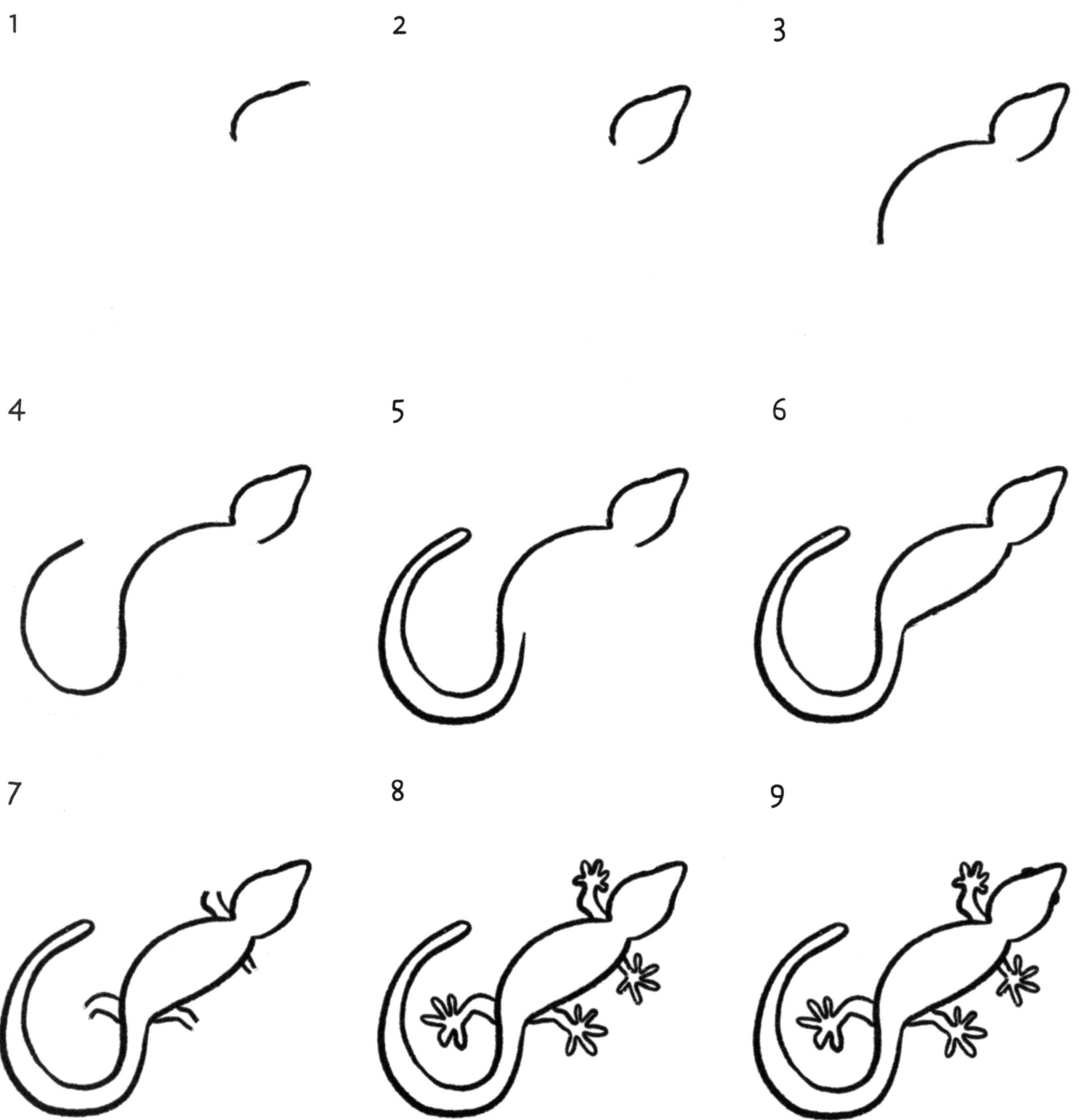

Slurp!
Geckos don't blink. They have a special clear covering on their eyeballs and lick them to keep them clean.

All About Geckos

★ Geckos can change the pattern of their skin for camouflage.

✱ Most geckos come out at night. They are able to see well in low light.

Trick tail
Geckos can shed their tails if they need to get away from a predator fast.

Superpowers
Geckos can climb anywhere because of tiny, sticky hairs on their feet.

How to Draw a Wolf

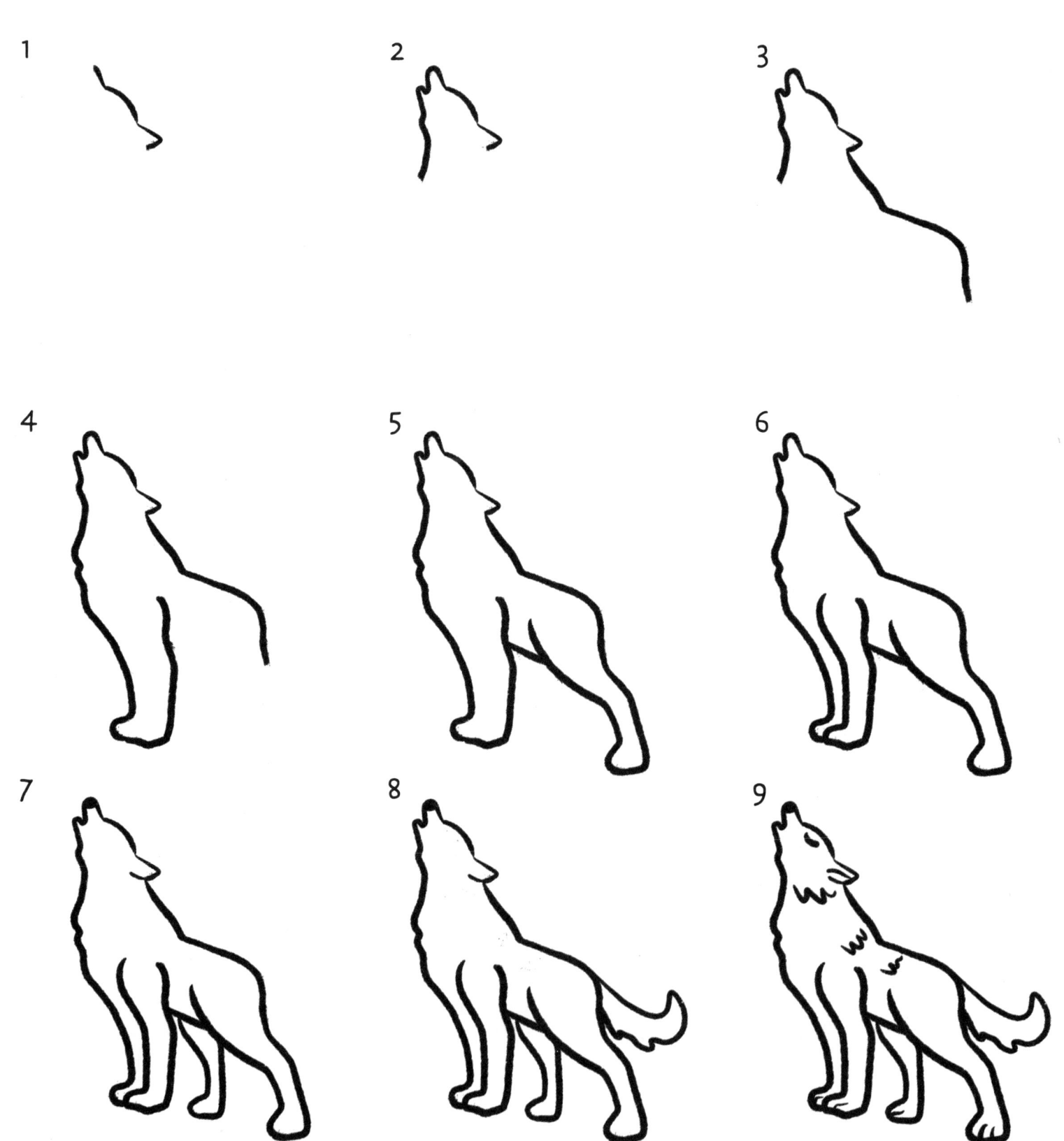

Awoooooo!
Howling is how wolves talk to each other over long distances.

All About Wolves

✶ Wolves can hunt large animals because they are good at working together in a pack.

★ Wolves can see, smell, and hear even better than dogs. They can smell 100 times better than humans!

Warm wolves
Wolves can live in really cold places because they have thick, fluffy fur.

Long legs
Wolves have long back legs. These help them run fast, even in deep snow.

How to Draw a Gorilla

All About Gorillas
- Gorillas are about the same height as humans, but 10 times stronger.
- Gorillas can make tools and even learn basic sign language.

Who's the boss?
The leader of a gorilla troop is called a silverback because he has silver fur on his back.

Funny face
When a gorilla opens its mouth without showing its teeth, that means it wants to play!

On all fours
Gorillas like to walk on their knuckles most of the time.

How to Draw a Seahorse

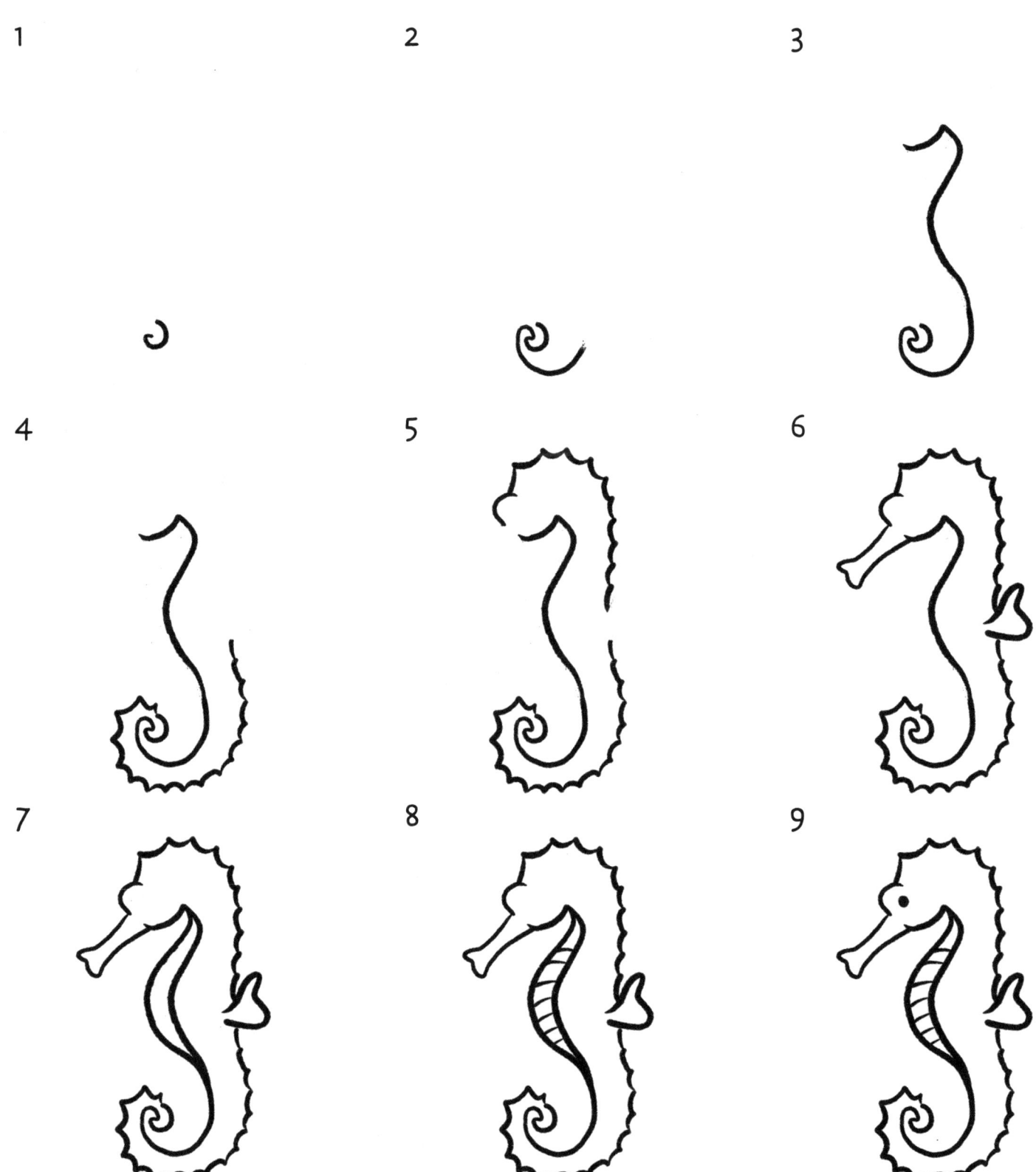

All About Seahorses

★ A seahorse steers through the water with its back fin. It moves up and down using an air bubble inside its body!

★ After the female seahorse lays eggs, the male keeps them in a special pouch until they hatch.

Sneaky snout
Seahorses use camouflage to hide from their prey. Then they suck it up through their snouts!

Tough skin
Seahorse skin is made of spiny plates to protect it from harm.

Time to rest
Seahorses can use their tails to hold on to coral.

How to Draw a Polar Bear

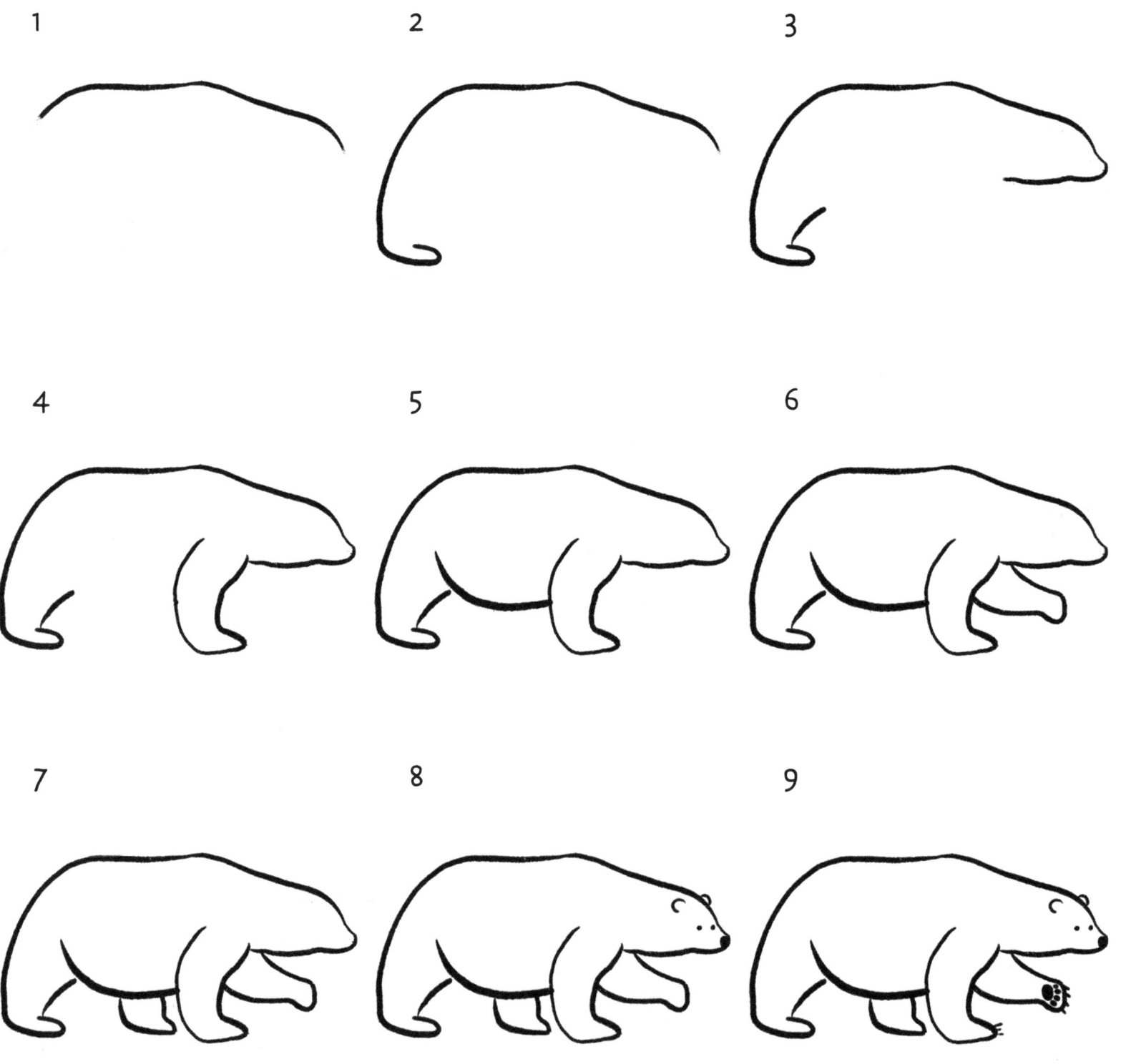

Big bears
A polar bear can be more than 2.5 m (8 ft) tall standing upright—about the height of a doorframe.

All About Polar Bears

★ A polar bear's skin is black under its white fur. The fur is for camouflage, while its black skin is for warmth.

✱ Polar bears are strong swimmers! They use their giant front paws to paddle through the water.

Super smell
Polar bears can smell animals up to 1.6 km (1 mile) away.

Extra grip
The pads on the bear's paws are covered in bumps to help it grip the ice.

How to Draw a Bat

1
2
3
4
5
6
7
8
9

Fabulous fliers
Bats are the only mammals that can fly.

Upside down
Bats sleep like this so that if a predator attacks, they can fly off right away.

Blind as a bat
Instead of their eyes, bats use their hearing to "see" the world.

Wings or hands?
Bat wings are like very thin, webbed hands, with four long fingers and a thumb.

All About Bats
* There are over 1,300 different bat species. That's a fifth of all the mammals on Earth!
* When it's flying, a bat's heart will beat up to 1,000 times a minute.

How to Draw a Rhino

1
2
3
4
5
6
7
8
9

Ancient animals
Rhinos have been around for millions of years.

Best friends
Oxpecker birds like to ride on rhinos. They eat bugs to keep the rhino's skin clean.

How many horns?
African rhinos like this have two horns. Other types have just one.

Keen ears
Rhinos can smell and hear very well.

All About Rhinos

★ Some rhinos live in groups called crashes!

✱ Rhinos love wallowing in mud. It's like natural sunscreen and helps protect them from insect bites.

How to Draw a Hedgehog

1
2
3
4
5
6
7
8
9

52

How to Draw a Tiger

1
2
3
4
5
6
7
8
9

How to Draw a Dolphin

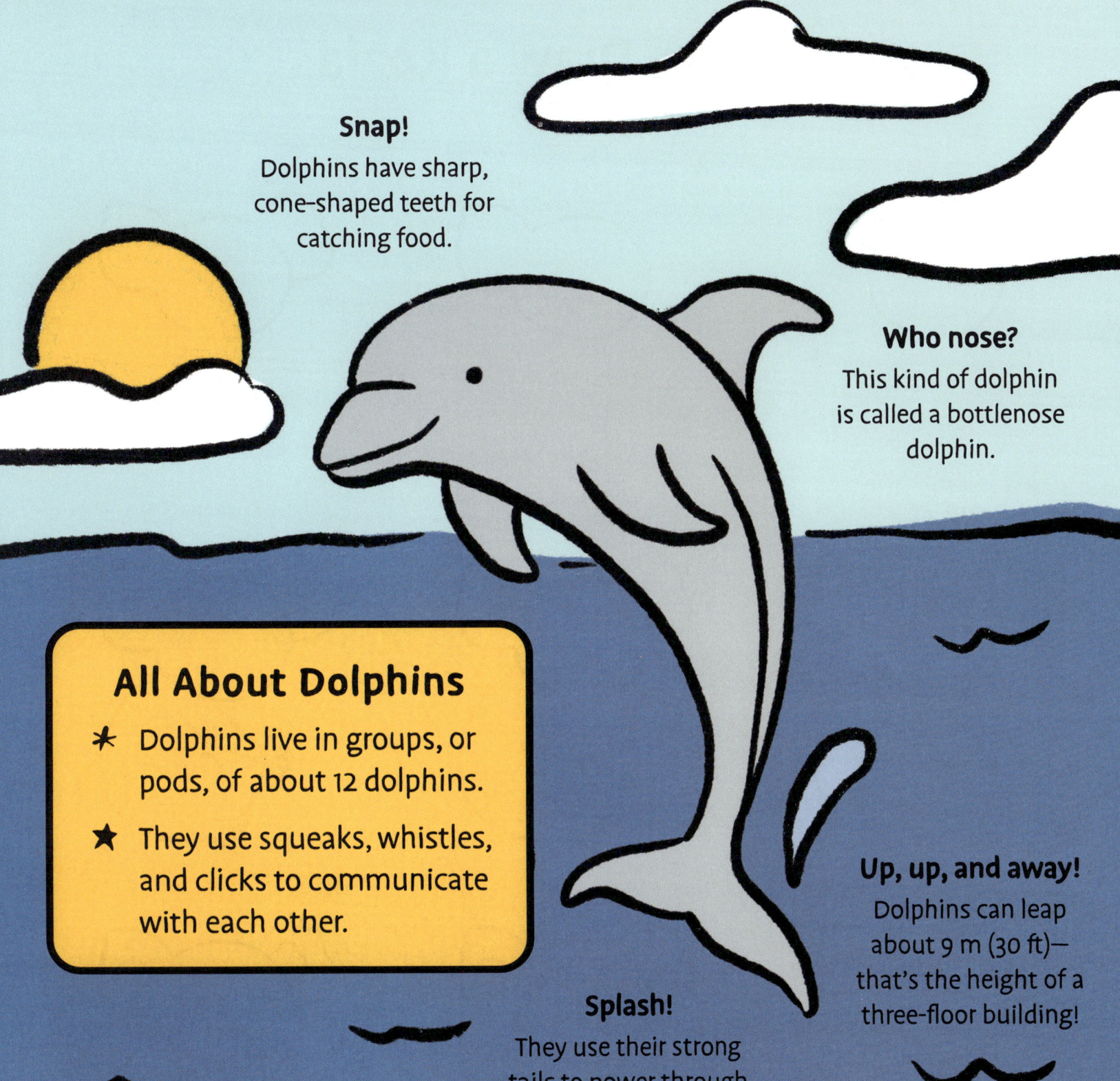

How to Draw a Koala

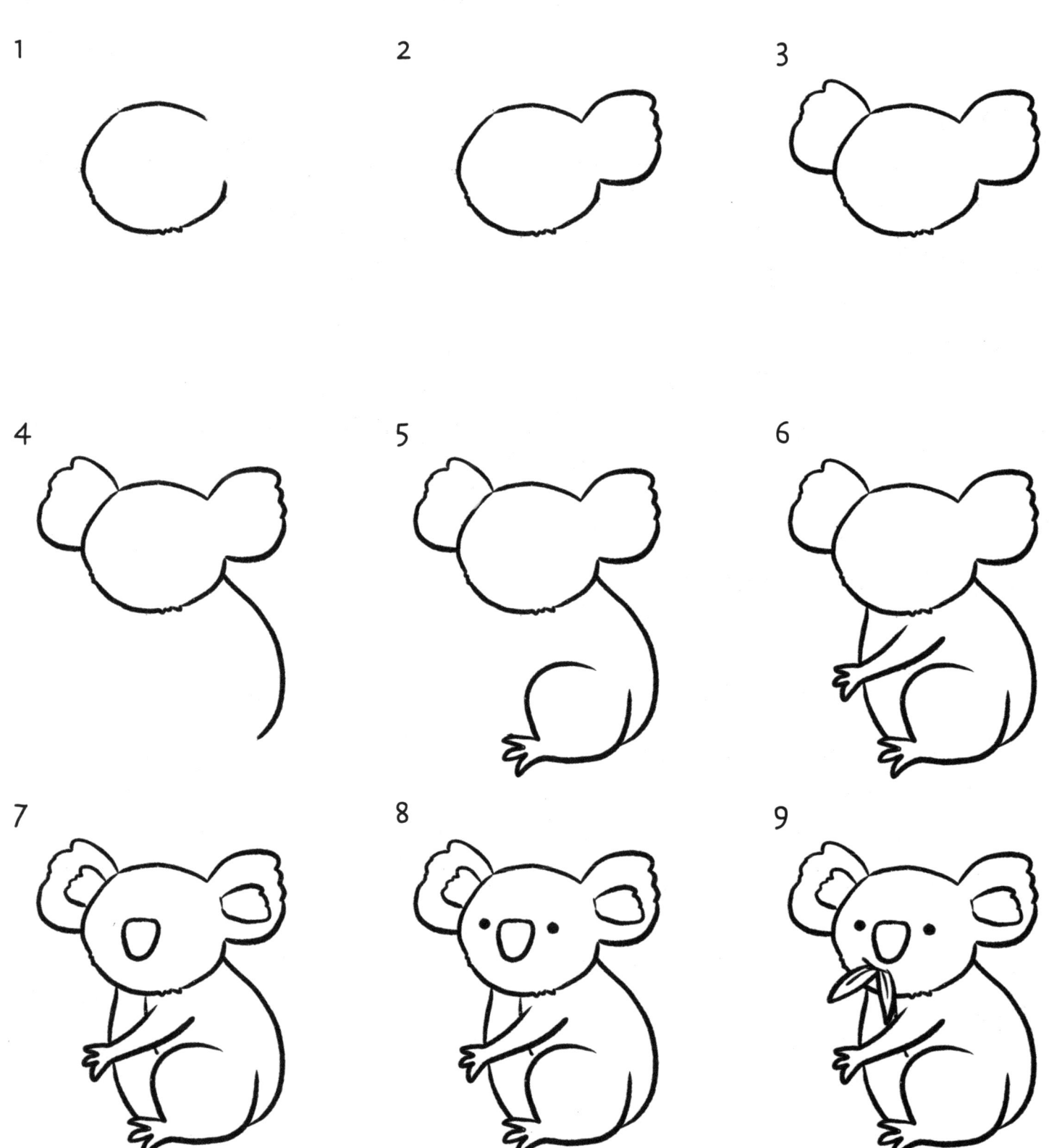

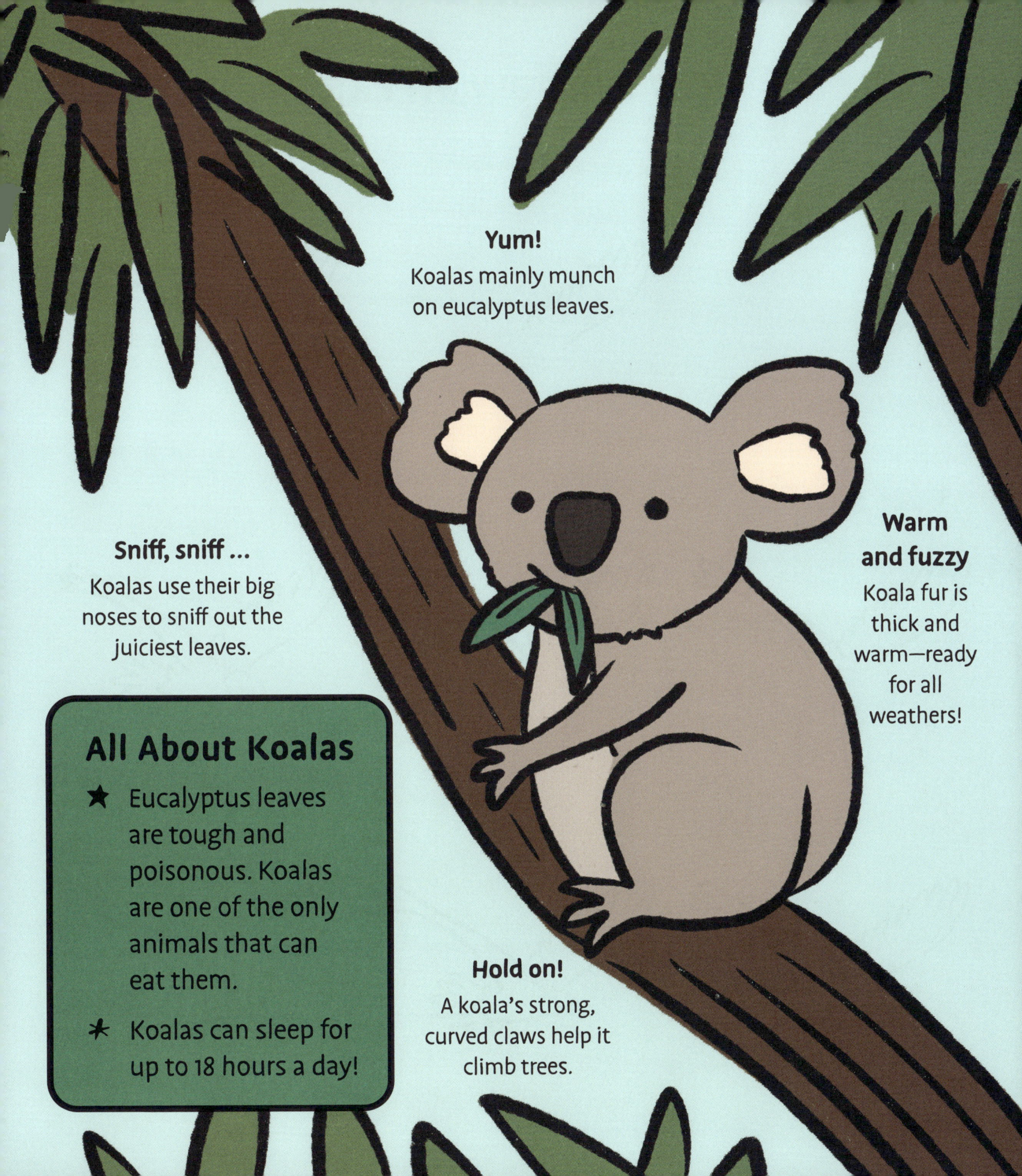

Yum!
Koalas mainly munch on eucalyptus leaves.

Sniff, sniff ...
Koalas use their big noses to sniff out the juiciest leaves.

Warm and fuzzy
Koala fur is thick and warm—ready for all weathers!

Hold on!
A koala's strong, curved claws help it climb trees.

All About Koalas

★ Eucalyptus leaves are tough and poisonous. Koalas are one of the only animals that can eat them.

★ Koalas can sleep for up to 18 hours a day!

How to Draw an Eagle

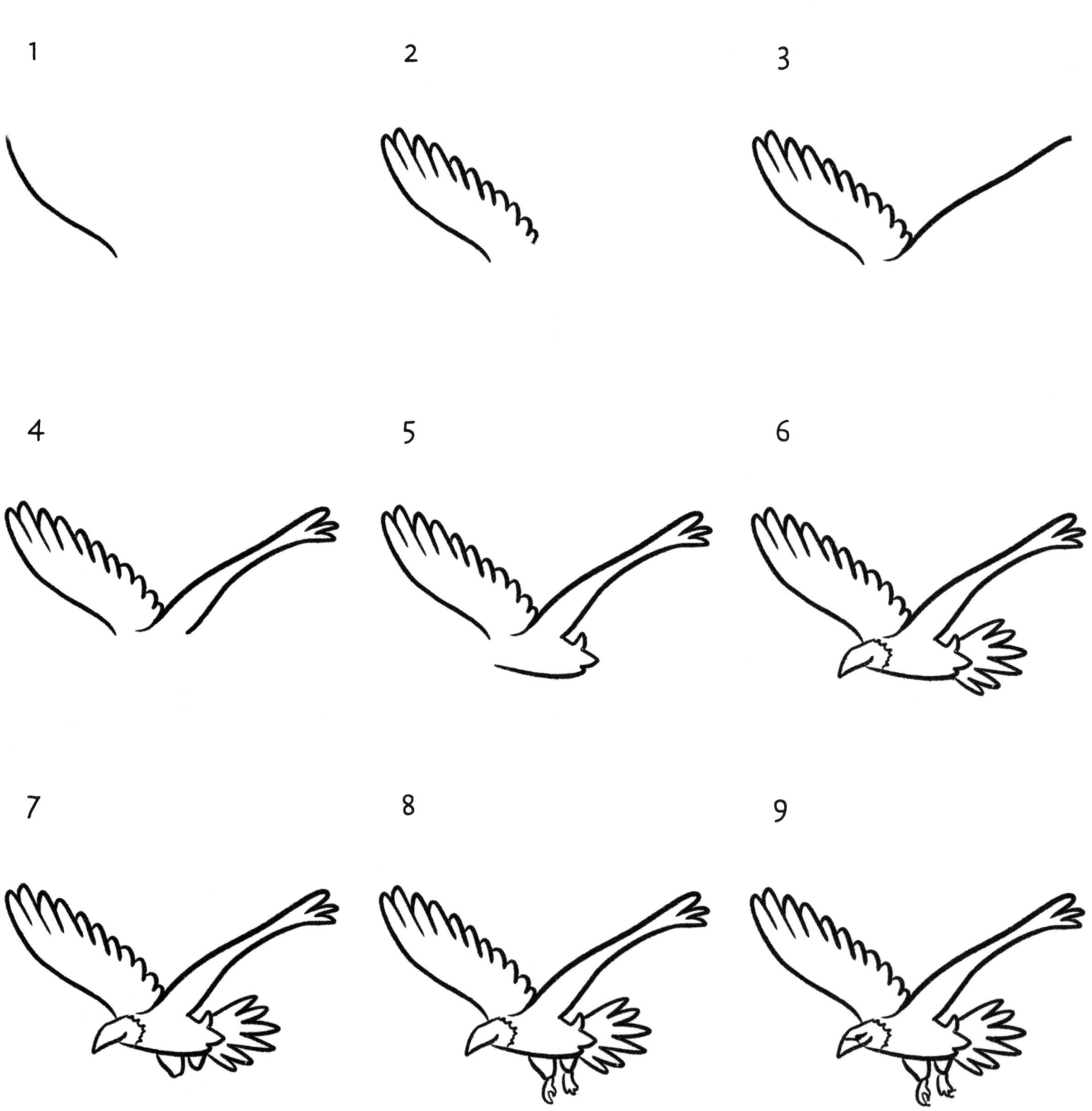

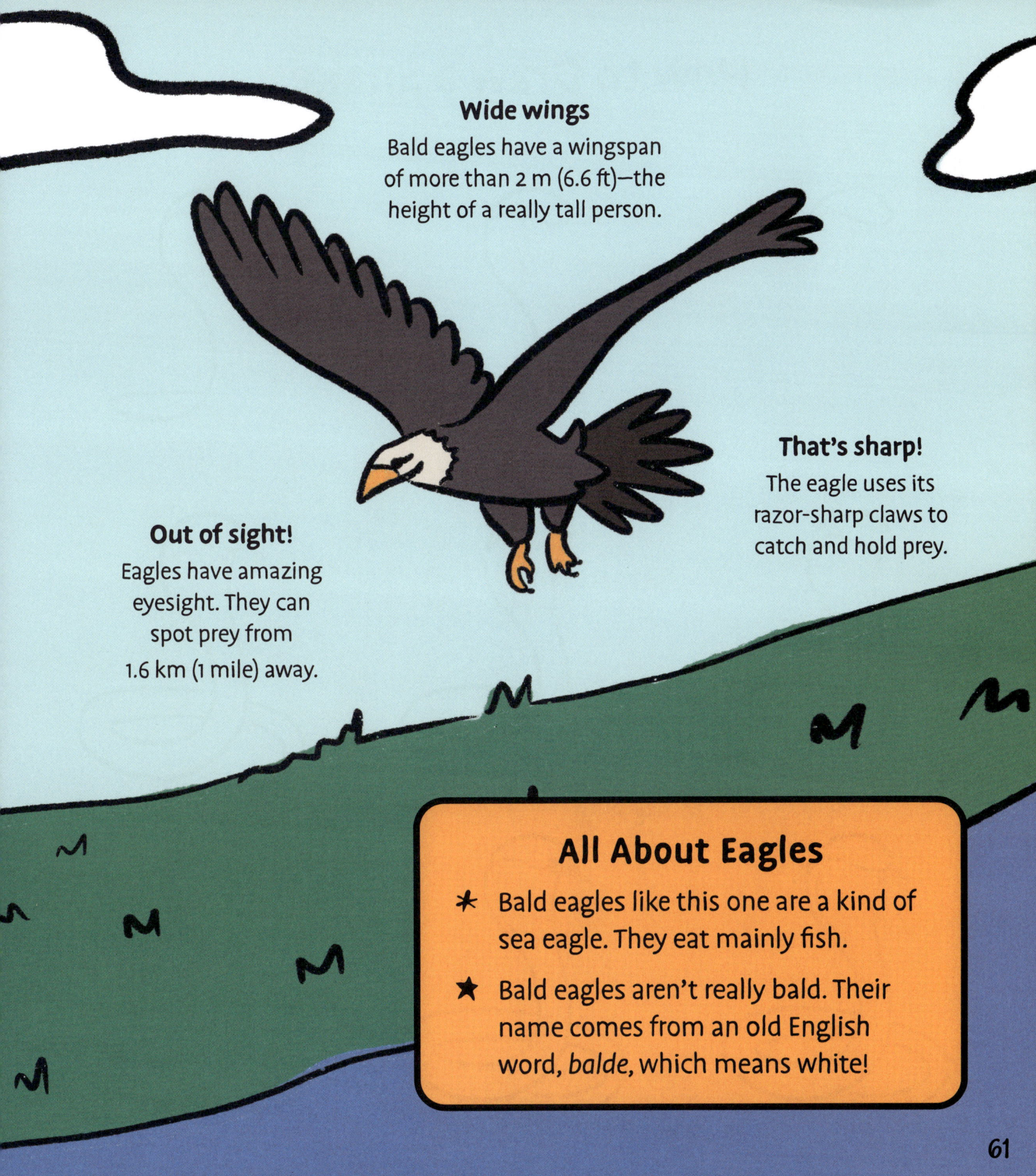

Wide wings
Bald eagles have a wingspan of more than 2 m (6.6 ft)—the height of a really tall person.

Out of sight!
Eagles have amazing eyesight. They can spot prey from 1.6 km (1 mile) away.

That's sharp!
The eagle uses its razor-sharp claws to catch and hold prey.

All About Eagles

* Bald eagles like this one are a kind of sea eagle. They eat mainly fish.

* Bald eagles aren't really bald. Their name comes from an old English word, *balde*, which means white!

How to Draw a Snake

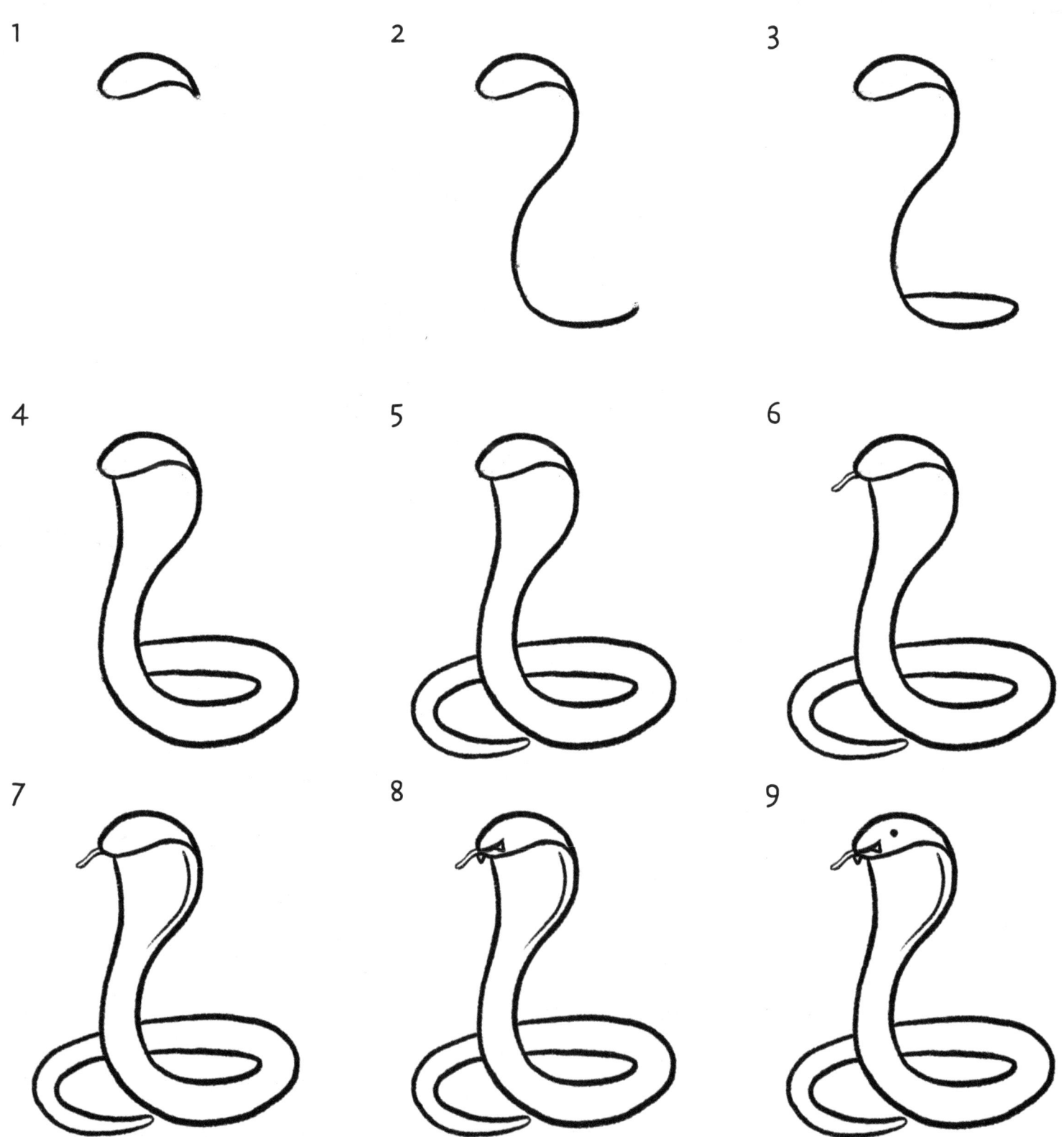

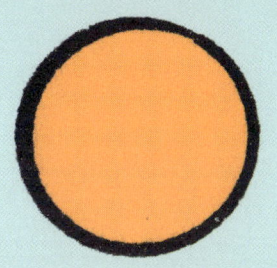

All About Cobras

★ King cobras can make a sound just like a dog growling.

✱ A single cobra bite has enough venom to kill an elephant.

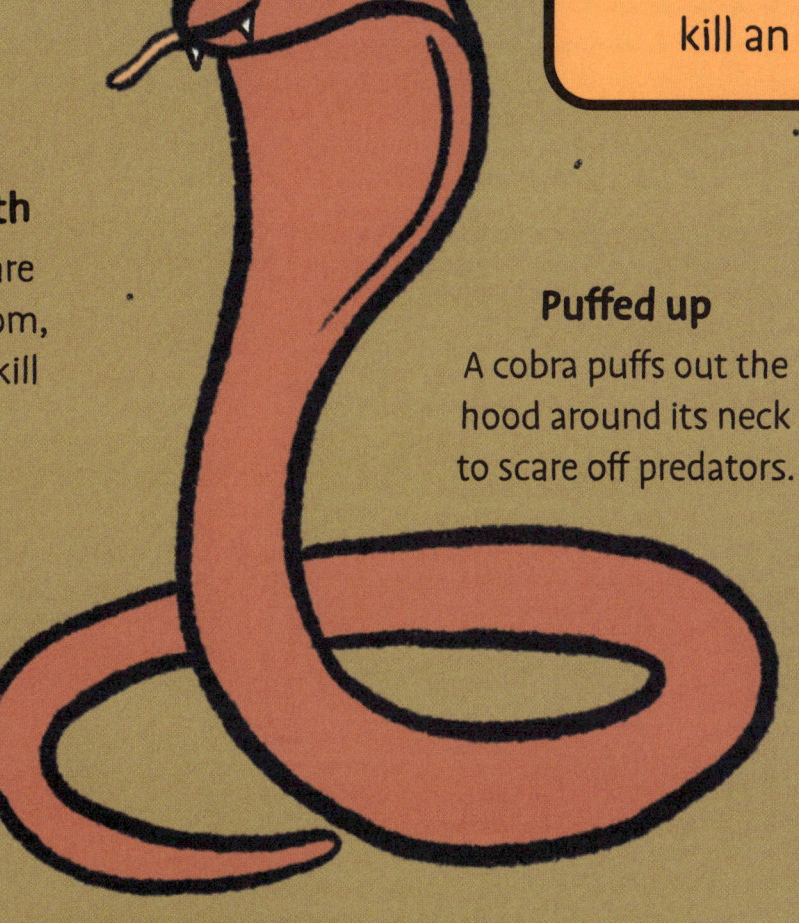

Monster mouth
A cobra's fangs are packed with venom, which it uses to kill its prey.

Puffed up
A cobra puffs out the hood around its neck to scare off predators.

Hungry snakes
King cobras eat other snakes and their eggs, as well as lizards, birds, rats, and mice.

Scaly skin
The snake's scales help it move smoothly over all kinds of surfaces.

How to Draw a Giraffe

1
2
3

4
5
6

7
8
9

Stre-e-e-e-etch!
Giraffes use their long necks to eat leaves from tall trees.

All About Giraffes

★ Giraffes are the tallest land animal. They can grow up to 5.5 m (18 ft) tall—a bit taller than the height of a basketball hoop.

★ They have long, purple-black tongues.

Camo coats
Each giraffe has a unique pattern on its coat for camouflage.

How to Draw a Rabbit

Wow!
Rabbits can turn their ears around to figure out exactly where a sound is coming from.

Bunny hop
Rabbits have strong back legs that help them jump really high!

All About Rabbits

★ Baby rabbits are called kits or kittens … just like cats!

✶ Rabbits dig underground homes called warrens.

Turn tail
Rabbit tails are white so that when they run away, other rabbits notice and run away, too!

How to Draw a Clownfish

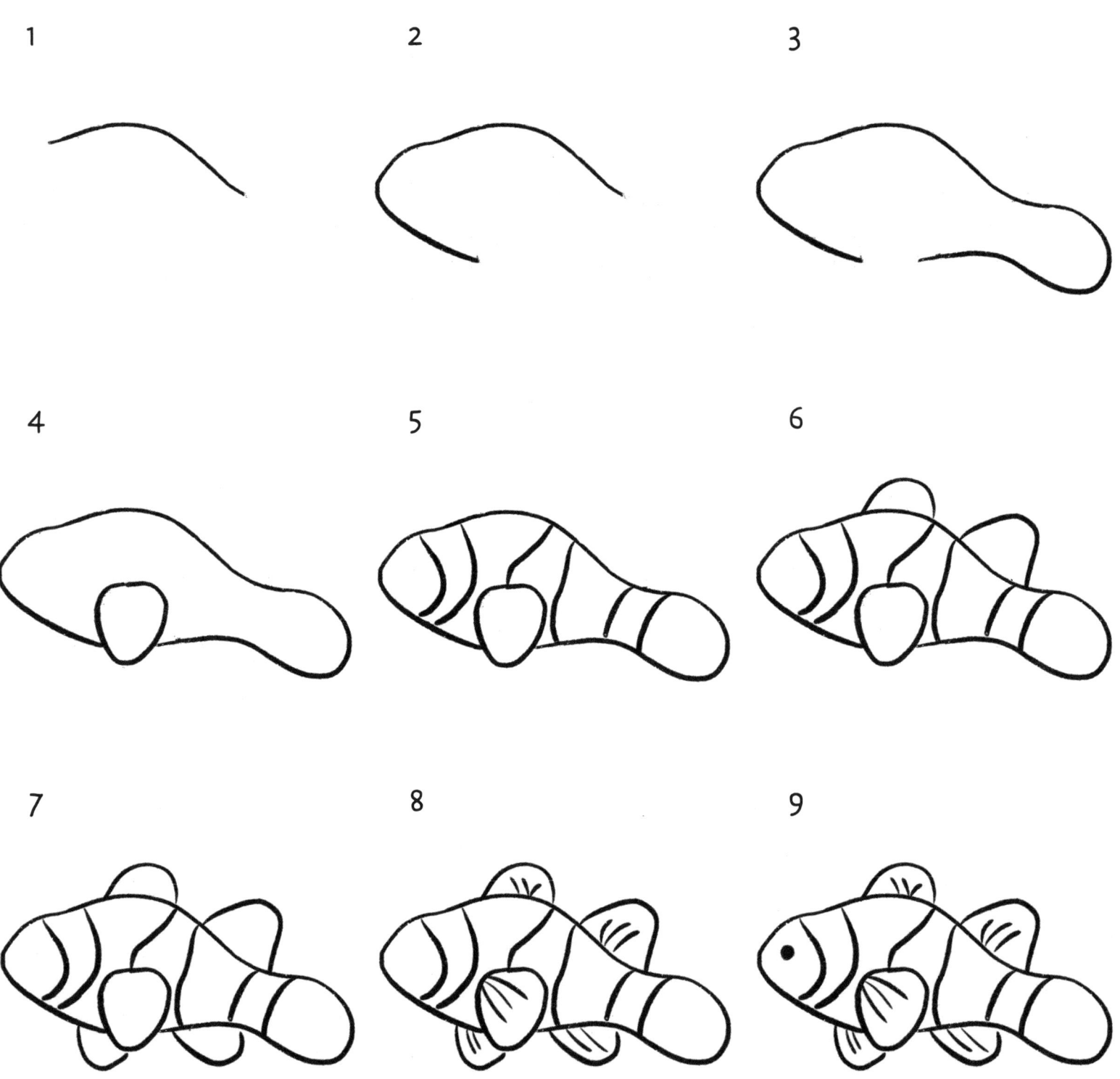

A happy pairing
Clownfish live among the stinging tentacles of sea anemones. These protect the fish. In return, clownfish provide food scraps for the anemones.

Male or female?
All clownfish are born male. Later, they can switch and become female.

Cute clowns
Clownfish are very small—about the size of a teacup!

All About Clownfish

* Clownfish talk to each other with popping and clicking noises!
* A layer of slimy stuff called mucus on the clownfish's scales protects it from anemone stings.

How to Draw a Raccoon

All About Raccoons

★ Raccoons are good climbers, swimmers, and fishers.

★ They have sensitive front paws, which they use to handle objects. They can even unlace shoes!

Mischief-makers
Raccoons look like they are wearing masks ... like bandits!

Nightlife
Raccoons mostly come out at night.

Fuzzy fur
A raccoon's fur helps it stay warm in cold weather.

How to Draw a Flamingo

How to Draw a Crab

1
2
3
4
5
6
7
8
9

Crab's-eye view
A crab's eyes are on stalks so it can see more.

Side shuffle
Crabs can walk in any direction ... but they prefer to move sideways.

How many?
Crabs have 10 legs, including their front claws.

All About Crabs

★ There are over 4,500 different crab types.

✱ Some types of crabs can shed their claws and grow new ones.

How to Draw a Horse

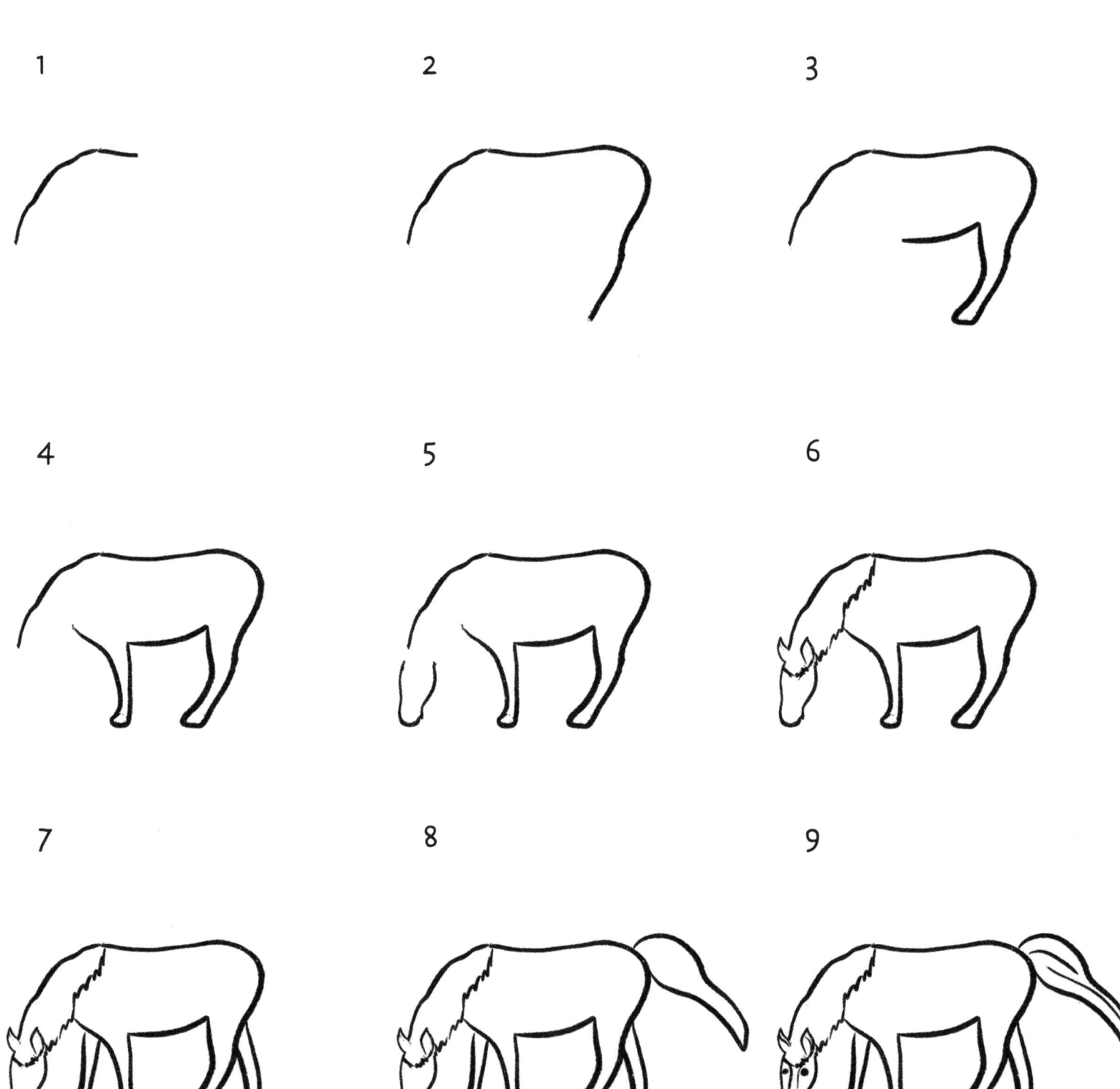

All About Horses

* There are around 60 million horses in the world today.
* Humans have been using horses for thousands of years.

Enormous eyes
Horses have bigger eyes than any other land mammal—and three eyelids!

Deep breath!
Horses can only breathe through their noses, not their mouths.

Super sleep
Horses can lock their legs in place and go to sleep standing up.

How to Draw an Ostrich

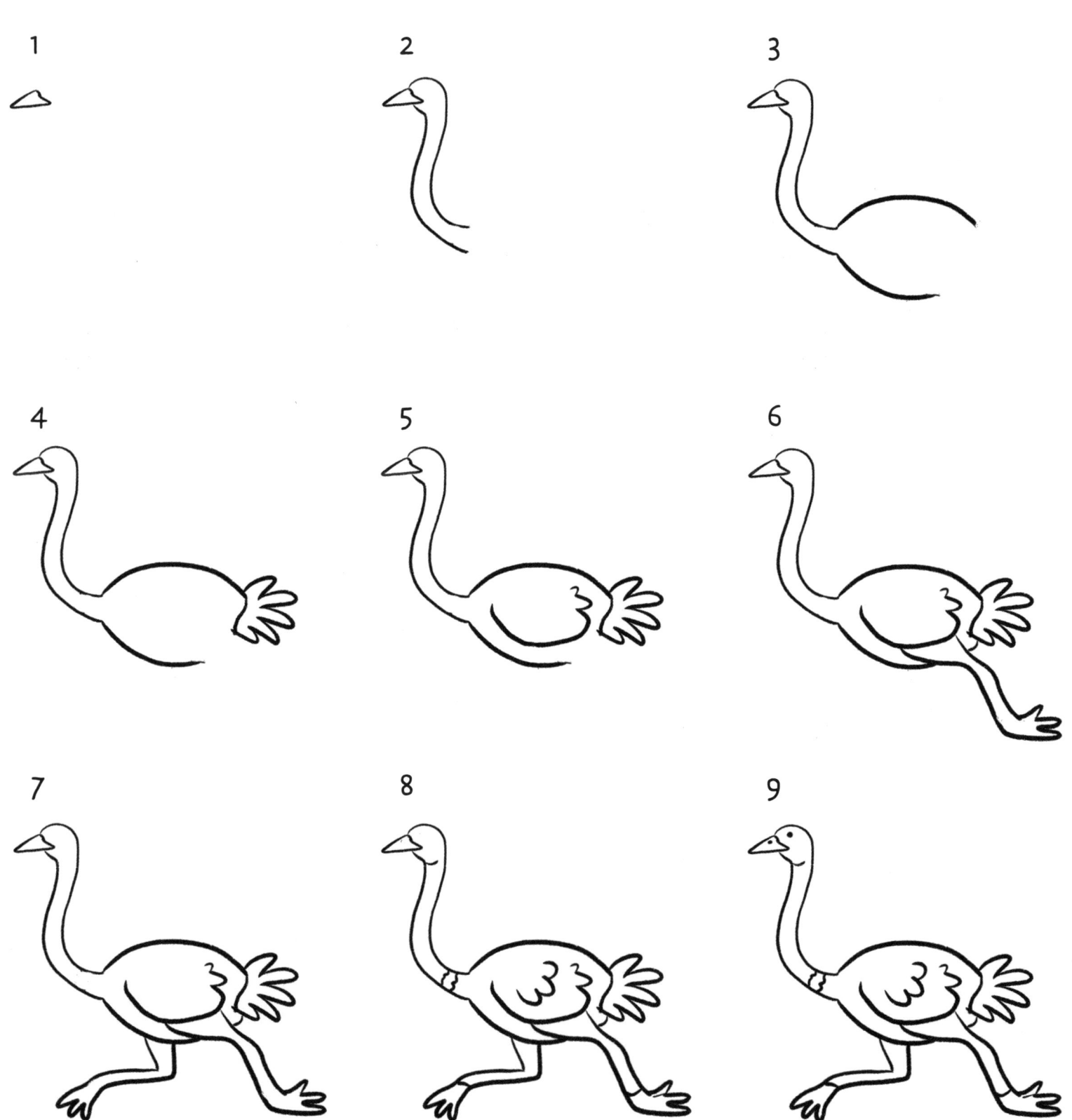

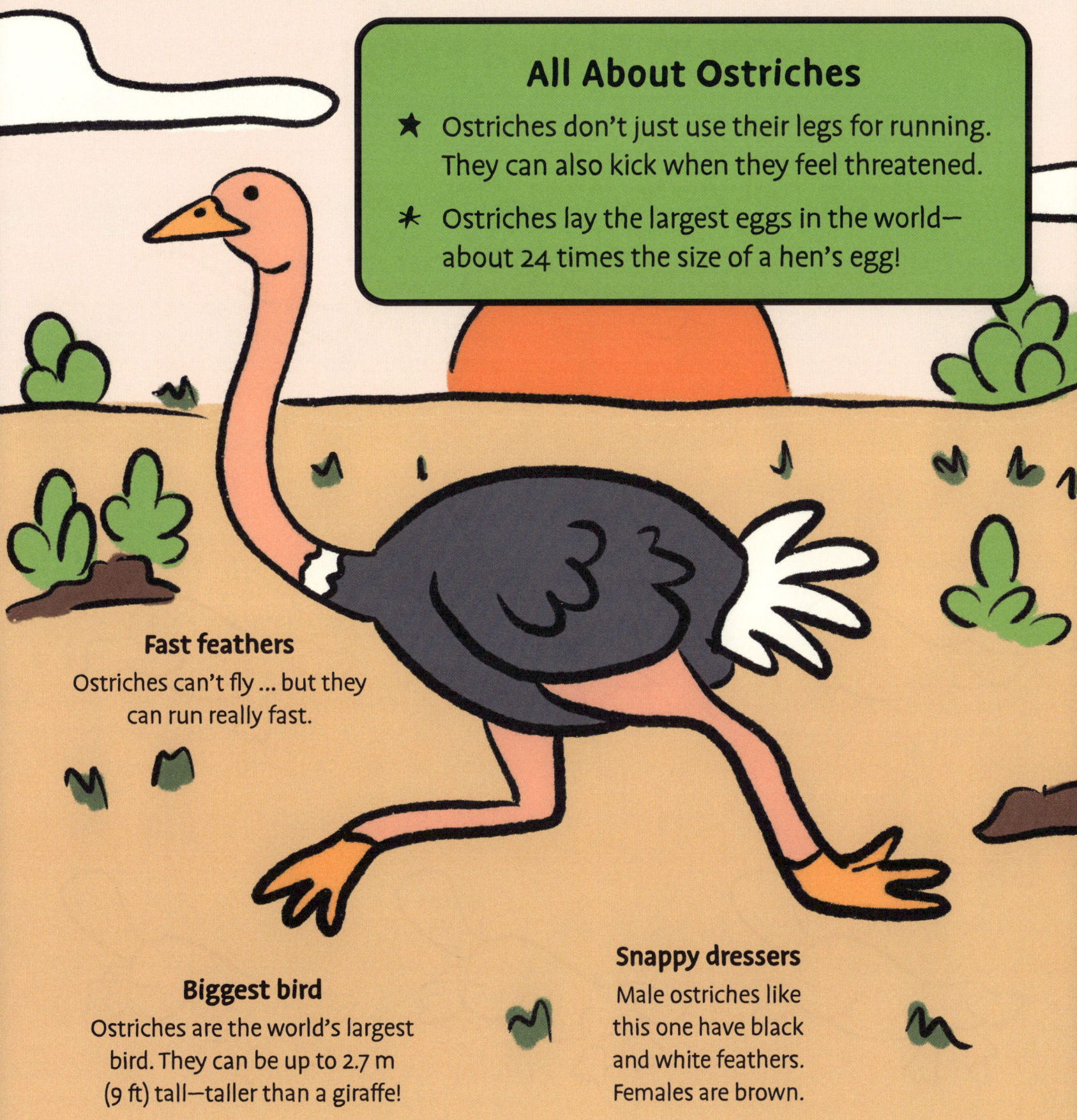

All About Ostriches

★ Ostriches don't just use their legs for running. They can also kick when they feel threatened.

★ Ostriches lay the largest eggs in the world—about 24 times the size of a hen's egg!

Fast feathers
Ostriches can't fly ... but they can run really fast.

Biggest bird
Ostriches are the world's largest bird. They can be up to 2.7 m (9 ft) tall—taller than a giraffe!

Snappy dressers
Male ostriches like this one have black and white feathers. Females are brown.

How to Draw a Platypus

1
2
3
4
5
6
7
8
9

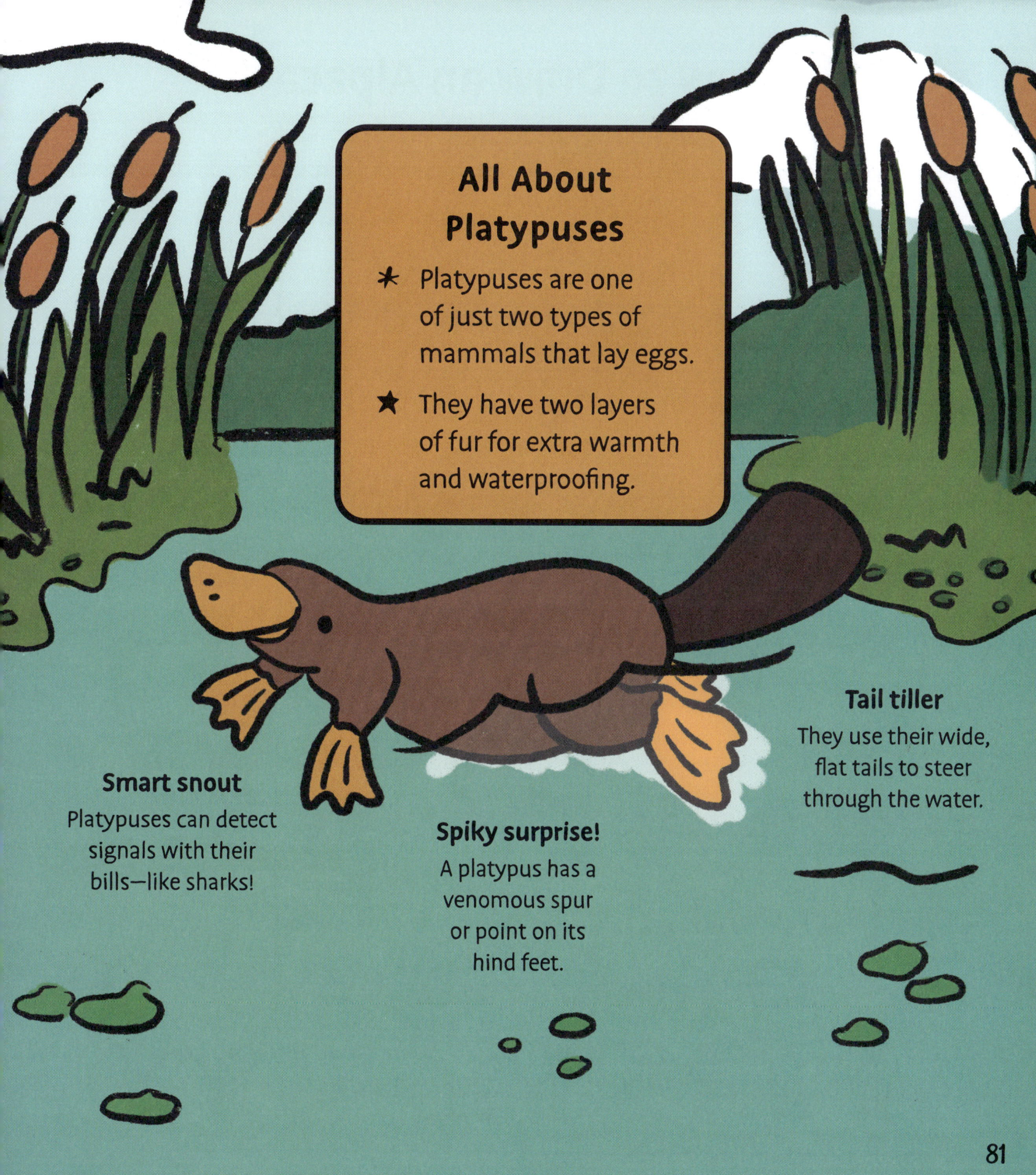

How to Draw an Alpaca

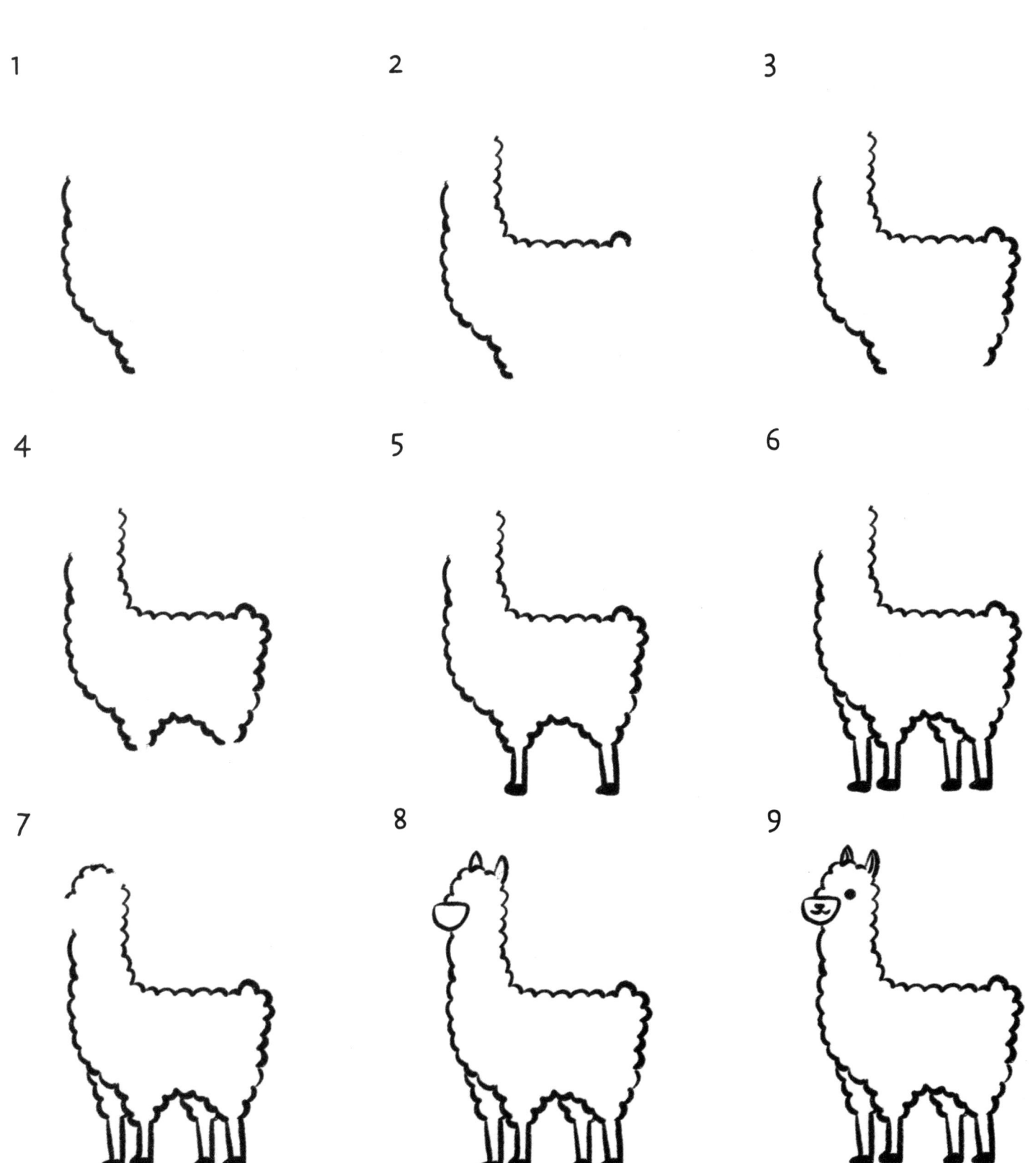

All About Alpacas

★ Alpacas look similar to llamas, which are larger and stronger.

✱ Humans have been farming alpacas for at least 6,000 years.

Spitting mad
When alpacas get angry, they spit!

Soft as clouds
Alpacas have warm, soft wool that is perfect for making cloth.

Tough toes
The alpaca has four toes on each hoof. This is useful for walking on stony trails.

How to Draw a Monkey

1
2
3
4
5
6
7
8
9

That's handy!
Monkeys have fingers and thumbs, like humans do.

Hanging out
Many monkeys, like this one, spend most of their time in the trees.

Talented tails
Monkeys use their tails to balance and hang from trees.

All About Monkeys

★ There are 264 different types of monkeys. That's a lot!

★ The smallest type of monkey is about the size of a banana. The largest is as big as a dog!

How to Draw a Turtle

1
2
3
4
5
6
7
8
9

All About Turtles

★ Turtles have been around on Earth for 200 million years.

✱ Even though turtles live at sea, they lay their eggs on land.

Snap!
Turtles have sharp beaks instead of teeth.

Safe shell
The turtle's shell acts as protection. It's really part of its skeleton!

Flip out
Turtles use their giant flippers to steer through the water.

How to Draw a Fox

All About Foxes

✱ Foxes dig dens, or "earths," underground. This is a safe place to raise their babies.

★ Foxes live in most places on Earth, from cities and forests, to deserts and the Arctic.

Let's chat!
Foxes use 28 different calls to communicate with each other.

Clever tails
Foxes use their tails to balance, stay warm, and signal to other foxes.

Turning red
Red foxes like this one are born with brown fur. They turn red when they are a month old.

How to Draw an Elephant

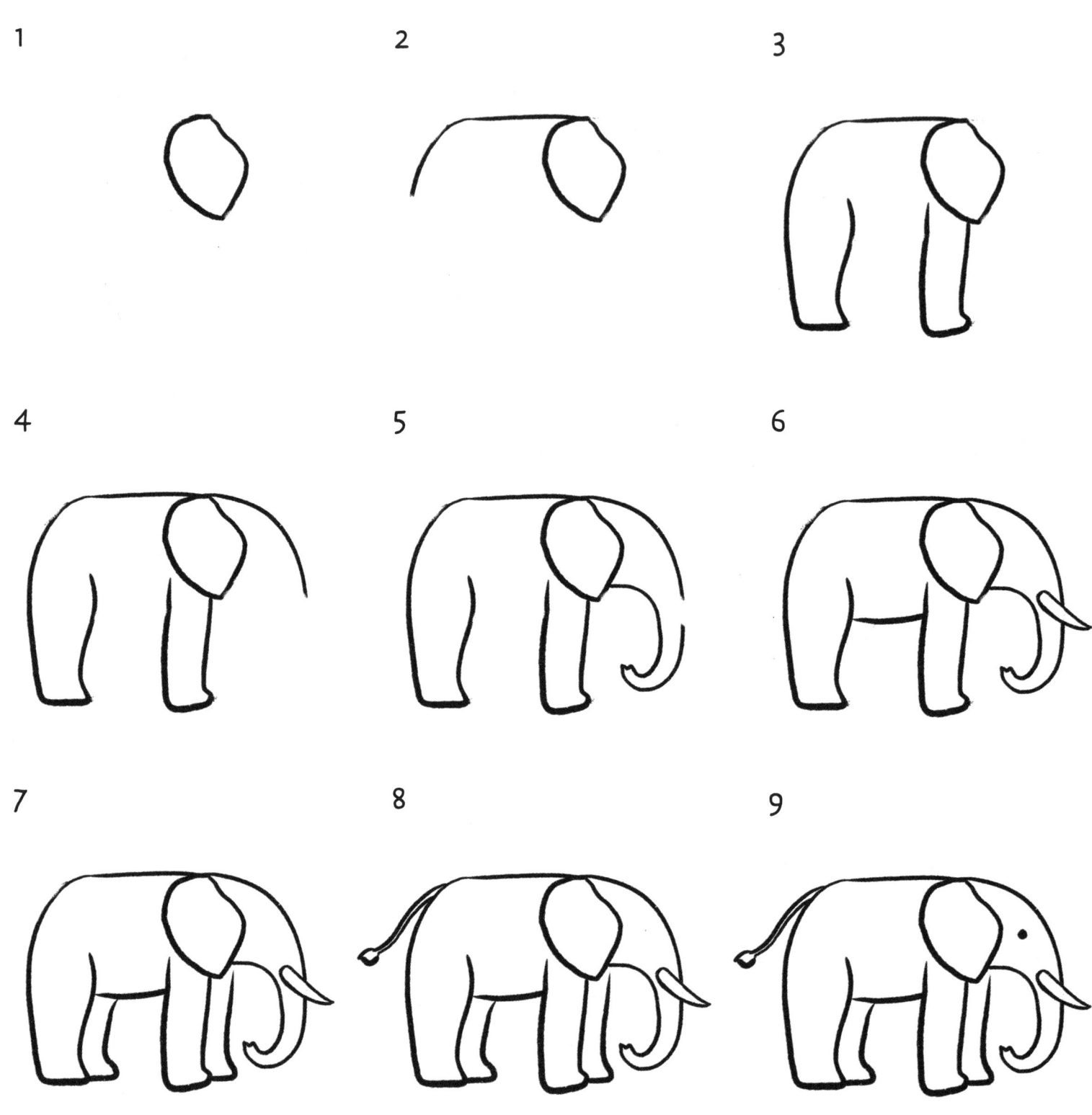

How old?
Elephant tusks never stop growing. The bigger the tusks, the older the elephant!

Wow!
Elephants have 150,000 muscles in their trunks.

All About Elephants

★ African elephants like this grow up to 3 m (9.8 ft) tall and can weigh 7,500 kg (16,500 lb)—the same weight as a small passenger plane!

★ Elephants spend up to 18 hours eating every day.

How to Draw a Beaver

All About Beavers

★ Beavers make walls called dams in rivers using sticks, logs, mud, and rocks.

★ They live near the dam, in a home called a lodge.

Warm and dry
Beavers have oily fur that is naturally waterproof.

Tough teeth
Beavers use their strong, sharp teeth to cut down trees, remove bark, and build dams and their homes.

Splish splash
They use their webbed feet and flat tails to swim fast.

How to Draw a Panda

1
2
3
4
5
6
7
8
9

All About Pandas

★ Baby pandas are pink, hairless, and about the size of a pencil!

Light and dark
Pandas have perfect camouflage: white for snow, black for shady areas.

Not so big ...
Giant pandas are actually just 1.5 m (5 ft) tall. That's shorter than most adult humans!

Hold on!
Instead of thumbs, pandas have extra-long wrist bones to help them grip food.

What an artist! You've learned how to draw animals from all over the world.

Do you know which animals live together in the same places? Try drawing a watering hole with elephants, giraffes, and zebras—or an underwater scene.

Or you could take your animals on a wild adventure. What about drawing a spaceship crewed by squirrels or a submarine full of sloths?

There are no limits when you know how to draw!